CONTENTS

■ ENGLAND'S ADMIRAL ■

ADMIRAL HORATIO Nelson is the greatest of all England's sailor heroes. The men he led followed him cheerfully and without question. He won important sea battles during the Napoleonic Wars against the French. His love for Lady Emma Hamilton was famous. And he died fighting at Trafalgar – the most famous sea battle in British history.

From the time he first went to sea, Nelson believed he would be an admiral and command a fleet in battle. He spent most of his life at sea in wooden sailing ships. He was often seasick and he was badly wounded – losing his right arm and the sight of his right eye. Even when in pain and unhappy, he was sure that he would win the biggest battle. His men respected and loved him: 'the Nelson touch' inspired loyalty.

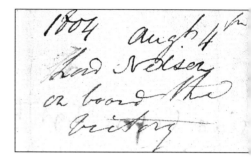

▲ The signature of Horatio Lord Nelson, England's greatest naval hero.

▼ A picture by Nicholas Pocock in which all of Nelson's most famous ship are shown at anchor at Spithead. HMS *Victory,* Nelson's flagship at the battle of Trafalgar, is on the far right. Behind her is the *Captain,* which he commanded at Cape St Vincent. To the left is *Elephant,* his flagship at Copenhagen, *Vanguard,* his flagship at the battle of the Nile, and *Agamemnon,* his first big ship.

NELSON'S LIFE

1758 Born.
1770 Enters the Royal Navy.
1771 Goes to sea as a midshipman.
1773 Sails to the Arctic.
1777 Becomes a lieutenant.
1778 Commands his first ship.
1787 Marries Frances Nisbet.
1794 War with France. Loses sight of his right eye during an attack in Corsica.
1797 Fights in the battle of Cape St Vincent. Leads attack on Santa Cruz, Tenerife, is wounded and has his right arm amputated.
1798 Defeats the French fleet in battle of the Nile.
1801 Battle of Copenhagen against the Danish fleet.
1803 Made commander-in-chief of the British Mediterranean fleet.
1805 Defeats French and Spanish fleets at Trafalgar. Dies.

■ BRITISH HISTORY MAKERS ■

HORATIO NELSON

LEON ASHWORTH

A Cherrytree Book

Designed and produced by
A S Publishing

First published 1997
by Cherrytree Press Ltd
a subsidiary of
The Chivers Company Ltd
Windsor Bridge Road
Bath BA2 3AX

© Cherrytree Press Ltd 1997

British Library Cataloguing in Publication Data

Ashworth, Leon
    Horatio Nelson. – (British history makers)
    1.Nelson, Horatio Nelson, Viscount – Juvenile literature
    2.Admirals – Great Britain – Biography – Juvenile literature
    3.Napoleonic Wars, 1800-1815 – Naval operations – Juvenile
        literature
    4.Great Britain – History, Naval – 19th century – Juvenile
        literature
    I.Title
    359.3'31'092

ISBN 0 7451 5290 2 (Hardcover)
ISBN 0 7540 9013 2 (Softcover)

Printed and bound in Italy by New Interlitho, Milan.

Acknowledgments

Design: Richard Rowan
Editorial: John Grisewood
Artwork: Malcolm Porter
Photographs: *Barnaby's Picture Library* 28/29 top, 29 bottom left *The
Bridgeman Art Library* 8/9 bottom (Christie's Images), 9 top left (Agnew &
Sons, London), 10 top (Agnew & Sons, London), 11 bottom (Bonham's,
London), 13 bottom (Yale University Art Gallery), 24 top (Lauros-Giraudon),
25/25 bottom (Phillips Auctioneers) *The Mansell Collection* 16 bottom *Mary Evans
Picture Library* 17 top right *National Maritime Museum* 4 top & bottom, 5 (&
cover), 6 top & bottom, 7 top left & right, 9 top right, 10 bottom, 11, 12 (& 1),
12/13 top, 14/15, 16, 17 top left & bottom (& cover), 18, 19, 20/21, 22/23, 25 top
& centre, 26/27 (& cover) 27, 28 bottom left, 29 bottom right

'He is so good and pleasant that we all wish to do what he likes, without any kind of orders'.
Captain George Duff of the *Mars*, one of Nelson's ships at the battle of Trafalgar.

'I will be a hero and, confiding [trusting] in Providence, I will brave every danger'.
Nelson, recovering from sickness in India, 1776.

◀ This portrait of Nelson was painted immediately after his victory at the battle of the Nile, which took place in 1798.

■ THE PARSON'S SON ■

HORATIO NELSON WAS born on 29 September 1758. Horace, as he liked to be called, was the sixth of 11 children born to the Reverend Edmund Nelson and his wife Catherine. Three children died as babies. The family lived in the rectory at Burnham Thorpe, a small village in Norfolk not far from the sea.

EVENTS

1756 *William Pitt (the Elder) becomes prime minister. Britain at war with France.*
1757 *British under Clive defeat French in India.*
1758 *Nelson born.*
1760 *George III becomes king.*
1762 *Catherine the Great becomes empress of Russia.*
1763 *James Watt builds his first steam engine. The Industrial Revolution affects the way people work, with new factory machines such as James Hargreaves' spinning jenny (1764).*
1767 *Nelson's mother dies.*

NELSON'S MOTHER

Nelson's mother's family were called Suckling, and among her ancestors was Sir Robert Walpole, Britain's first prime minister. This made her rather grander than Nelson's father, whose grandfather had been a baker. She died in 1767 when Nelson was only nine years old.

A COUNTRY CHILDHOOD

As a country parson, Nelson's father was not a rich man. He grew his own vegetables to help make ends meet. Yet he was able to keep two menservants, and paid village women

▲ Nelson at the age of eight.

▼ The Old Rectory at Burnham Thorpe, Norfolk, where Nelson was born and lived as a child. He could be the small boy waving a flag in the picture.

to cook, clean and care for the younger children.
The family lived quietly. News from outside travelled
slowly, for letters and newspapers had to come over
dusty roads from London by coach and wagon.

BOYHOOD HEROES

The most exciting news of Nelson's boyhood was
of Britain's war with France – the Seven Years'
War (1756-1763). His boyhood hero was
General James Wolfe, who captured
Quebec in Canada from the French
but died at the moment of victory.
He read of battles in India won
by Robert Clive, and of other
British victories at sea.

▲ Nelson's mother died when he
was only nine. His grandmother
helped to look after him and saw
him off to join the navy.

▶ Nelson's father was a kind but
strict man. It must have been
hard for him to cope on his own
with so many children.

RULING THE WAVES AND THE WORLD

IN NELSON'S day, Britain,
France, Spain and Portugal
all had empires in far-flung
parts of the world. From their
colonies they earned great
wealth which gave them
power at home in Europe, so
they were constantly trying to
outdo each other. To gain and
manage the colonies, naval
power was essential. The navy
transported troops to fight on
land, and protected the
overseas possessions and
merchant ships. Holding on to
colonies and to power was
not always easy. In Nelson's
lifetime, Britain was to fight a
war against its own subjects in
America, while France was to
experience a revolution that
brought Napoleon Bonaparte
to power, and plunged Europe
into war.

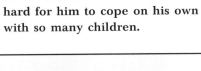

NORTH AMERICA

GREAT BRITAIN NETHERLANDS

FRANCE

PORTUGAL SPAIN

ASIA

AFRICA

SOUTH AMERICA

AUSTRALIA

Main European
colonies in 1763

British

Spanish

Portuguese

Dutch

French

▶ James Wolfe, like
Nelson, died in the
hour of victory when he
captured Quebec in 1759.

■ SCHOOLDAYS ■

EDMUND NELSON was a pious but strict father. The children had to sit up straight at table, with their backs not touching the chair. Horatio was soon sent away to school, as was usual with the sons of clergymen.

Horatio attended three schools in Norwich, Downham Market and North Walsham. At this last school, he is said to have crept out at night to pick pears from the headmaster's garden. He gave the pears to his friends, and enjoyed their admiration.

AN AMBITION TO DO WELL

Two of Nelson's brothers became clergymen. Another worked as a clerk in the Navy Office in London. His sisters married and made their own homes. But Horatio had his sights set on the world beyond England. Days spent watching ships sailing along the coast near home may have made him dream of the sea and joining the navy. He had an uncle – his mother's brother – who might

NAPOLEON

NAPOLEON Bonaparte (right) was born 11 years after Nelson, in 1769. While Nelson's boyhood was peaceful, Napoleon's was full of drama. Napoleon was born on the Mediterranean island of Corsica, where his father was fighting for its independence from France. By 1804 Napoleon had made himself emperor of France and master of Europe. The biggest block to further French victories was Britain's Royal Navy and Nelson – the parson's son from Burnham Thorpe.

▲ Captain Maurice Suckling – the brother of Nelson's mother – helped and encouraged his nephew to join the navy.

help. In 1770 Captain Maurice Suckling was made commander of a 64-gun battleship. Britain was making ready for a possible war with Spain. Nelson asked his brother William to write to their father, who was staying in Bath. 'Tell him I should like to go to sea with my uncle Maurice'. Nelson had decided where his destiny lay.

◀ A coastal scene from Nelson's time. The boy learned about the sea and ships while watching and talking to local fishermen, but it was the great sailing ships that maintained Britain's power and wealth that stirred his imagination.

■ THE YOUNG MIDSHIPMAN ■

NELSON WAS ONLY 12. His uncle Maurice joked: 'What has poor Horatio done, who is so weak, that he should be sent to rough it out at sea?' It was no joke. Life at sea in the 1770s was tough. All the Nelson children seem to have been rather delicate and Nelson was small for his age. He might not survive.

HIS FIRST SHIP

Still Nelson would go. In 1771 he left Norfolk. His father went with him as far as London, and then said goodbye as the boy took the stagecoach for Chatham, in Kent. There, in the naval dockyard, Nelson found his uncle's ship. Workmen were busy patching her up in case of war.

Uncle Maurice was not yet on the ship, so Nelson had to make himself at home as best he could. A kindly officer bought him dinner at an inn. That night he slept in a hammock for the first time, in the overcrowded cabin he shared with the other midshipmen.

▲ **Captain Phipps commanded the expedition to the Arctic in 1773, in which Nelson served on the *Carcass***

▼ **Nelson fearlessly raises his gunbutt to club a wounded polar bear. He was determined to take the animal's skin home as a trophy. Luckily for him, a cannon shot from the ship scared the bear away.**

A MIDSHIPMAN'S LIFE

THE MIDSHIPMEN on a warship were junior officers, but they could be any age from 13 to over 40. As a newcomer, Nelson got the worst jobs. He worked alongside the ordinary seamen (right), learning to climb to the mast top, to haul on ropes and sails, and handle a small boat. The midshipmen breakfasted like the ordinary sailors on 'burgoo', a thick porridge, and dished out soup and stew from a huge tin dish. They lived in a cheerful muddle. There was no privacy and no one was very clean.

WIDENING HORIZONS

Nelson did not stay long aboard the battleship. There was no war. So, to give the lad a taste of the wide ocean, Captain Suckling sent him on a merchant ship to the West Indies. Nelson was seasick crossing the Atlantic. All his life, he was seasick on any vessel smaller than a battleship. But he loved life at sea.

Nelson was lucky to have his uncle to help him. In 1773, now almost 15, he joined an expedition to the Arctic. Other young officers were left with boring jobs ashore. No sooner was he back from the Arctic than he was sailing in a new ship to India.

▼ A view of Greenwich and Deptford in London, showing the Royal Dockyard in 1789. Over 12,000 workers were employed in building and repairing the navy's huge fleet of over 800 ships, making this Britain's biggest industry.

INDIA, SICKNESS AND WAR

Nelson spent almost two years in the East, until he became sick at the end of 1775. He was so ill that he had to be shipped home. During the six-month voyage, he slowly regained his strength. He landed at Woolwich to hear the news that Britain was at war.

■ TAKING COMMAND ■

BRITAIN WAS AT war with its own subjects, people who had settled in America and founded colonies on the east coast. The American colonists had rebelled against the British government. They said it was unfair for Britain

▶ **The newly promoted Captain Horatio Nelson looked healthy but was in fact often ill. He suffered bouts of yellow fever and scurvy, as well as sea-sickness.**

MANNING THE FLEET

THE ROYAL Navy in the 1700s was always short of men. Some men went to sea willingly, hoping for adventure and treasure. But many sailors were at sea only because they had been seized by the press-gang – a kidnap squad sent out to gather recruits (below). Men

were hauled off merchant ships at sea or in port. Others were grabbed from the street or tavern – often drunk or unconscious. The hapless men awoke to find themselves at sea.

to tax the American colonies when they had no say at all in how Britain was governed. The Americans had no navy to threaten Britain. But France and Spain did, and these two countries backed the American rebels. The Royal Navy had to protect merchant ships and stop aid from reaching the Americans.

PROMOTION AND HIS FIRST SHIP

In the spring of 1777, Nelson passed his examination to become a lieutenant. He wrote to his brother William, 'So I am now left in the world to shift for myself, which I hope I shall do . . .'

The new lieutenant was gaining experience. He sailed on convoy escort to Gibraltar and led a press-gang to collect recruits for the fleet. Captain Suckling had died, but Nelson had caught the eye of senior officers. In 1778 he was made commander of a small warship called *Badger*, and sailed to the Caribbean.

AN ILL-FATED MISSION

Nelson's orders were to lead a land expedition through the jungles of Nicaragua. He was to attack a Spanish fort and seize all the gold he could find. The mission ended in near-disaster: local guides ran away, and seamen hauling boats and guns overland became exhausted and sick. Nelson showed courage and determination, but it was not enough. He was taken back to Jamaica suffering from yellow fever, and complaining (as he often did) that he was very ill.

◆ The Boston Tea Party of 1773 was an early incident in the American Revolution. The colonists objected to paying taxes to Britain for goods landed in America. Disguised as Native Americans, they threw cargoes of tea overboard into Boston Harbour.

■ NEW EXPERIENCES ■

T HE WAR IN America was going badly for Britain. But it was being lost by politicians and soldiers, not by sailors. Nelson went off to holiday in Bath. He was still sure that he would command a fleet.

Nelson's next voyage took him north to the Baltic Sea. He sailed in the *Albemarle*, a captured French ship. The French built the finest warships of the day, and the Royal Navy had a number of French vessels. Nelson fell ill with scurvy, a disease caused by poor diet that affected many seamen in the 1700s. Then, he sailed to Canada and saw Quebec, the fort-city where his boyhood hero James Wolfe had died.

A USEFUL FRIEND

Nelson met Prince William (later King William IV) who was also in the navy. The young prince thought Nelson quaint for a captain – very young-looking, with his lank hair tied back, and wearing an old-fashioned waistcoat. Nelson thought the prince would be a useful friend in high places.

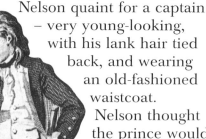

◀ **Nelson met and became friendly with Prince William Henry, the future King William IV (the 'sailor king'), shown here as a midshipman.**

▶ **Nelson leaves the *Lowestoff* in rough seas to board a captured American ship in November 1777, during the American Revolution.**

DISCIPLINE AT SEA

D ISCIPLINE on naval ships was strict. Punishments included floggings – being beaten on the bare back with a knotted rope known as the 'cat-o'-nine-tails' (right). The worst crime was mutiny – refusing to obey orders. In 1797 seamen at the navy bases of Spithead and the Nore mutinied, demanding better conditions. The leaders of the protest were hanged.

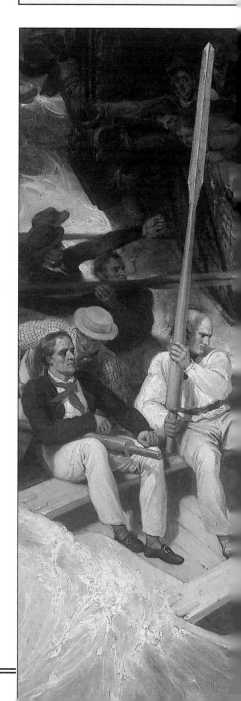

▲ Pictures that Nelson (left) and Cuthbert Collingwood made of each other in 1785. After meeting in the West Indies, the two young officers became lifelong friends and rose to be admirals.

SURE OF HIMSELF

Deciding he must learn French, Nelson spent some time in France, where he also enjoyed the company of English girls he met. Then he was ordered to the West Indies, to help prevent trade with the newly independent Americans. Nelson was so keen on this task that he upset local merchants and one island governor, who asked whether such a young officer knew what he was doing. Nelson retorted that 'he had the honour to be as old as the prime minister of England' (William Pitt, who was only 24).

MRS NELSON

On 11 March 1787, Nelson married Frances Nisbet, a doctor's widow who kept house for her wealthy uncle on the Caribbean island of Nevis. She had a small son, Josiah. The wedding took place on the island. Then the new family returned to England.

Norfolk winters came as a shock to Mrs Nelson, who was used to tropical warmth. Shivering, she stayed in bed, wrapped in curtain material. Downstairs, Nelson studied sea charts, browsed through books about the sea, or read the newspaper to his father, whose sight was now weak. Home life bored Nelson, who was no gardener or sportsman. The countryside in winter usually gave him a cold. He was restless, waiting for action. Great events were shaping.

◀ Nelson's wife Frances (Fanny) Nisbet was used to the warm Caribbean. She and her five-year-old son found their first Norfolk winter cold and dull.

▲ King Louis XVI executed by guillotine in 1793 during the French Revolution. So began the 'reign of terror', during which France declared war on Austria, Britain and Prussia.

◀ Admiral John Jervis commanded the British fleet that roundly defeated the Spanish at Cape St Vincent in 1797. He greatly admired Nelson.

▼ Nelson leads a boarding party on to the *San Josef* during Spain's defeat in battle off Cape St Vincent in 1797. His part in the victory made Nelson the talk of the navy.

Vincent, off the southwest tip of Portugal. Spain was on the side of France. Jervis attacked.

Nelson – now on the 74-gun *Captain* – took his ship out of the line, drawing heavy gunfire from the enemy. The badly damaged *Captain* crashed into a Spanish ship and Nelson led his men in hand-to-hand fighting with swords and pistols. They captured the enemy ship, then boarded another.

A week later, Nelson was made a rear-admiral.

■ WOUNDED IN BATTLE ■

T HE NAME OF Nelson was on everyone's lips, and people stopped him in the street to shake his hand. The young admiral was soon to earn further honours. In July 1797, in his latest ship, the 74-gun *Theseus*, Nelson attacked the Spanish port of Cadiz. During the hand-to-hand fighting, a brave shipmate twice parried sword thrusts that might have killed Nelson.

NELSON LOSES HIS ARM

Two weeks later, Nelson was fighting off Tenerife in the Canary Islands, then a Spanish fortress. Nelson and his men rowed ashore in small boats. The Spanish fought bravely. During the landing, many sailors died and Nelson's right arm was shot through.

The British gave up. Some officers ate a quiet dinner with the Spanish, as both sides gathered their dead and wounded. That night, the ship's surgeon cut off what was left of Nelson's arm. He was given the drug opium to ease the pain, but was back at work within the hour. Struggling to hold the pen in his left hand, he wrote gloomily, 'the sooner I get to a very humble cottage the better

▲ **This picture of Sir Horatio Nelson, now a rear-admiral, was painted in Naples in 1799, shortly after the battle of the Nile.**

EVENTS

1797 *Nelson attacks Cadiz in Spain and Tenerife in the Canary Islands (July) and returns to England (September). Austria surrenders to Napoleon (October).*
1798 *Nelson joins Vanguard (March).*

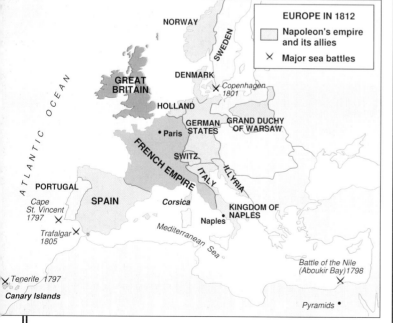

EUROPE IN 1812
☐ Napoleon's empire and its allies
✕ Major sea battles

NORWAY
SWEDEN
GREAT BRITAIN
DENMARK
✕ Copenhagen 1801
HOLLAND
GERMAN STATES
• Paris
GRAND DUCHY OF WARSAW
FRENCH EMPIRE
SWITZ.
ITALY
ILLYRIA
ATLANTIC OCEAN
PORTUGAL
Cape St. Vincent 1797 ✕
SPAIN
Corsica
KINGDOM OF NAPLES
Naples
Trafalgar ✕ 1805
Mediterranean Sea
Battle of the Nile (Aboukir Bay) 1798 ✕
✕ Tenerife 1797
Canary Islands
Pyramids •

SURGERY AT SEA

S HIPS' SURGEONS operated on wooden tables, painted red (so the blood would not show). They used knives and saws to amputate legs and arms. In some cases a wooden 'peg leg' could be fixed to the stump. Wounded men were given rum or opium to make them drowsy and dull the terrible pain while the surgeon was at work. Nelson complained that the coldness of the knife was painful, and suggested that surgeons heat their instruments.

and make room for a better man . . .'.

SIR HORATIO

When Nelson returned to England, he was made a
Knight of the Order of the Bath. He now had enough
money to buy a large house in the country. But his
arm healed slowly. People meeting him were shocked
by his grey hair, bad teeth and thin face.

Time for rest at home was brief. In
March 1798, Nelson was back at sea in the
Vanguard. The French had
gathered a fleet and an
army led by the young
General Bonaparte. An
invasion was coming. But
where? Nelson was to
seek out the enemy and
bring them to battle.

▼ Nelson wounded at
Tenerife in the Canary
Islands. As he stepped
ashore at Santa Cruz
harbour to seize
Spanish ships – and in
the act of drawing his
sword – his right arm
was shattered by a
musket ball. He was
rowed back to his
flagship and that night
the arm was
amputated at the
elbow.

■ INTO ACTION ■

IN 1793 NELSON took command of his first big battleship, the 64-gun *Agamemnon*. With him was his new servant, Tom Allen. Nelson's stepson, Josiah Nisbet, now 13, also joined the ship. After five years ashore, Nelson was happy to be back at sea.

NAPLES

Nelson sailed to the Italian port of Naples, where his ship anchored in the great bay beneath Mount Vesuvius. The king of Naples was needed as an ally in Britain's war against France. Nelson met the king and Sir William Hamilton, the British ambassador. The ambassador's attractive wife, Emma, was 'a young woman of amiable manners', wrote Nelson in a letter to his wife.

BATTLE SCARS

Nelson soon found the action he wanted. While fighting the French off the island of Corsica, he was hit by stones and splinters from a bursting cannon ball. His right eye was badly damaged; after this, he could see only light and dark with it.

In the scorching Mediterranean heat, Nelson made his sweating gun crews practise their shooting. This training had its reward when two French ships were damaged and captured.

Nelson felt the navy was not doing enough. He hoped that Admiral Sir John Jervis, newly in command of the British fleet, would win the much-needed victory.

CAPE ST VINCENT

On 14 February 1797, the British fleet met a larger Spanish fleet near Cape St

EVENTS

1793 *King Louis XVI of France and Queen Marie Antoinette are executed. Britain and France go to war.*
1794 *Corsicans seek Britain's help against France. Nelson loses the sight of one eye. In France, Danton and Robespierre, leaders of the revolution, are executed. Semaphore signal system is used in France.*
1795 *France introduces the metric system.*
1796 *Napoleon Bonaparte conquers most of Italy for France. Dr Edward Jenner discovers that inoculation protects people from smallpox.*
1797 *Mutinies of seamen at Spithead (Portsmouth) and the Nore (Thames). Battle of Cape St Vincent (14 February). Nelson promoted to rear-admiral.*

▶ Sir William Hamilton, the British ambassador to Naples. His young wife, Emma, fell in love with Nelson and later set up home with him.

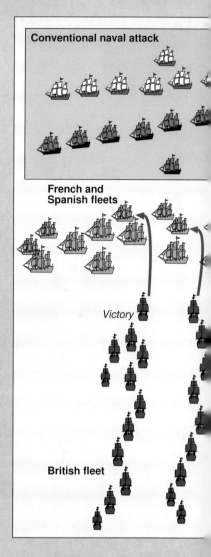

Conventional naval attack

French and Spanish fleets

Victory

British fleet

▲ At the battle of Trafalgar Nelson attacked in two lines, so cutting off the enemy centre before the leading ships could get near enough to help. This was a brilliant tactic. In classic 'old' sea battles (top) the fighting fleets drew up in lines facing each other and fought broadside to broadside.

SHIPS OF THE LINE

THE BIGGEST warship of Nelson's time was the ship of the line – so named because fleets usually sailed into battle in a line. Ships were 'rated' by the number of guns and men they carried: a first-rate vessel carried over 100 guns and up to 900 men. Smaller ships called frigates and sloops scouted to find the enemy and carried messages.

■ FIRST GREAT VICTORY ■

THE BRITISH FLEET lost touch with the French when their ships were scattered by a gale that damaged Nelson's ship. As soon as the repairs were made, Nelson set out eastward, searching the Mediterranean. Where was Napoleon going to land? Nelson and the British government both guessed: Egypt. Nelson duly found the French warships anchored in Aboukir Bay, near Alexandria. Napoleon was ashore. He had already beaten the Turks and Egyptians at the battle of the Pyramids. Now it was Nelson's turn.

THE BATTLE OF THE NILE

The water in Aboukir Bay was shallow and daylight was fading, but Nelson ordered his ships to sail boldly towards the French. Guns flashed in the darkness. Nelson's head was grazed by gunfire but, bandaged, he returned to the deck. After a 12-hour battle, the burning French flagship *L'Orient* exploded. The 'glorious victory' left Napoleon's army stranded in Egypt.

EVENTS

1798 Irish nationalists rebel against British rule in Ireland (May-June). Napoleon wins the battle of the Pyramids (21 July). Nelson wins the battle of the Nile (August) and is made Baron Nelson of the Nile (November).
1800 Robert Fulton, an American inventor, shows off his submarine Nautilus *to the French Navy. Washington D.C. becomes the new capital of the United States of America. Alessandro Volta makes the first electric battery.*

A SAILOR'S DAY

THE DAY AT sea began at 4 o'clock. Hammocks, slung from hooks between the guns, were stowed away. Breakfast of oatmeal porridge was washed down by 'Scotch coffee' (burnt biscuit mixed with boiling water). Dinner at noon was usually boiled salt pork or beef, with ship's biscuit, followed by a plain boiled pudding or duff. The men drank beer or grog (rum weakened with water), since

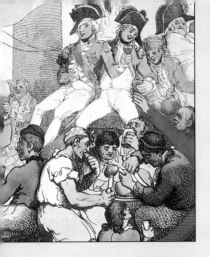

▲ Nelson celebrates with his crew after the battle of the Nile.

water in wooden barrels soon went bad. Biscuits often had weevils (insects) in them, and a man nibbling cheese (a rare treat) kept an eye out for wriggling worms. Supper was biscuit and pea soup. During the day, the gunners practised firing their cannon. Seamen scrubbed decks and scrambled aloft to set or bring in sails, or drilled in fighting with cutlasses (swords) and muskets.

ENGLAND'S HERO

Nelson was made a baron and granted a yearly pension of £2000 (then a huge sum) by the government. Bonfires blazed and bells rang. Pictures of Nelson were sold from street barrows, songs were sung about him, and a dance was named 'Vanguard'. The heroic admiral was in no hurry to return home. His ship needed repairs, and he felt tired and ill. He decided to revisit Naples.

WELCOME TO NAPLES

Lady Hamilton greeted the news of the battle by first fainting and then riding through Naples wearing a 'Nelson and Victory' headband. She welcomed the hero with open arms and gave a grand party for his birthday. But the celebrations were cut short. The French and their allies were coming! Mobs jeered in the street as the king of Naples and his guests fled to Nelson's ship and sailed for Sicily. The grateful king gave Nelson a new title: Duke of Bronte (a town on the slopes of Mount Etna). After this, he always signed his name 'Nelson and Bronte'.

▲ Nelson kept a copy of this portrait of Emma Hamilton in his cabin aboard ship.

▼ The battle of the Nile. The French fleet lies at anchor in Aboukir Bay. As dusk and Nelson's ships approach, the French open fire.

▲ A watercolour of the estate and country house at Merton that Emma Hamilton converted into a mansion.

▼ A visiting card, a single left-hand glove and a combined knife and fork used by Nelson after he lost his right arm.

visited wounded sailors and met a man who had lost an arm, like him. He said with a smile, 'Well Jack, you and I are spoiled for fishermen'.

A COUNTRY GENTLEMAN

Britain and France made peace in 1802. Nelson and Lady Hamilton set up home at Merton Place in Surrey, a 100-year-old country house. Nelson could afford to take care of his two sisters and of family servants, including James Price, a black man who had worked for his uncle Maurice. Nelson made his first speech as a member of the House of Lords. It seemed his sailor's days might be behind him.

▼ Danish (left) and British ships in action at the battle of Copenhagen.

BATTLE AT SEA

WHEN lookouts spotted enemy ships, drummer boys beat 'to quarters'. This was a signal understood by everyone. Sails and decks were soaked with buckets of water, so they would not catch fire easily. Wet sand was scattered so men would not slip on the decks. The cannon – normally roped down, to stop them rolling about – were freed and the gun ports (window-like openings in the ship's side) were opened. Out of each one, a cannon pointed, with its gun crew ready. The galley fire was put out and the surgeons prepared to deal with the wounded and dying. Everyone on board was silent. In six minutes the ship was ready for battle.

■ BRITAIN VERSUS NAPOLEON ■

BY 1801, BRITAIN felt alone against Napoleon, who was master of France and much of Europe. It seemed that Russia, Prussia, Sweden and Denmark might join with Napoleon. Nelson's thoughts, however, were on personal matters. He and his wife were no longer living together and in January 1801 Lady Hamilton had a baby daughter – named Horatia, after her father.

TURNING A BLIND EYE

This event delighted Nelson. But he was impatient for action. He was pleased to sail to Denmark, to attack the Danish fleet in port at Copenhagen. The enemy ships were defended by guns on shore, but Nelson led the British ships in close to bombard them. Hyde Parker, the fleet commander, signalled him to break off the attack. Nelson put his telescope to his blind eye and said, 'I really do not see the signal'.

Nelson called Copenhagen his hardest battle. After three hours, the two sides agreed a truce. Nelson

▲ Horatia, daughter of Nelson and Emma Hamilton, with her rocking horse in the garden at Merton in Surrey where Nelson and Emma set up home in 1802.

■ BEFORE TRAFALGAR ■

IN MAY 1803, the brief peace ended. Britain declared war on France. After Horatia's christening, Nelson travelled to Portsmouth to prepare for battle again. He was the new commander-in-chief, and had a new ship, the *Victory*.

The fleet spent much of 1804 waiting for the French ships to leave port. By the end of the year, Spain had joined the war. Nelson knew he would face a stronger and combined enemy.

FIND THE ENEMY

No French army could land in Britain while the Royal Navy kept watch on French ports. Nelson spent almost two years (June 1803 to July 1805) at sea. He ate little and slept badly, often rising in the dark to walk on deck in his stockinged feet.

In the spring of 1805, Admiral Villeneuve, the French commander, led his fleet across the Atlantic Ocean to the West Indies. Nelson followed but Villeneuve slipped back homeward. By August, both the French and Spanish fleets were in the Spanish port of Cadiz.

THE BATTLE NEARS

Nelson enjoyed a month at home in

▲ Napoleon Bonaparte crowned himself emperor of France in 1804. He planned to invade England, if only his fleet could decoy the British ships away long enough for his army to cross the Channel in barges.

▼ HMS *Victory* in Portsmouth Harbour, 1892. The famous ship is now in dry dock and open to the public.

▶ Nelson explains the plan of attack to his officers before the battle of Trafalgar. His courage put heart into his men: 'I am of the opinion that the boldest measures are the safest', he once wrote.

▼ Thomas Masterman Hardy was at Nelson's side on the *Victory*. He was captain of the ship and a close friend, usually cutting up Nelson's meat for him at dinner.

England, knowing that the great battle was not long off. On 15 September, he sailed from Portsmouth, after a grand farewell dinner on board *Victory*. He had paid his bills and planned next year's planting in the gardens at home. Crowds cheered and wept as he was rowed out to the *Victory*, waving his hat. In the coach taking him to Portsmouth he had written a prayer in his diary, beginning 'May the great God, whom I adore, enable me to fulfil the expectations of my country . . .'

HMS *VICTORY*

THE *VICTORY* had a crew of nearly 1000 men. Their average age was 22. The most experienced seamen were in charge of the huge iron anchors and the sails at the front of the ship that were important for steering. To lift an anchor from the seabed needed the muscle-power of about 250 men turning a winding wheel called a capstan. Topmen (70 sailors to each mast) climbed the tall masts to take in and release the main sails. Other men worked on deck, hauling on ropes. On each of the three gun decks were from 28 to 32 guns, evenly divided between the two sides of the ship. The *Victory* had 104 guns in all. The biggest guns could shoot a ball through oak planks 60 centimetres thick at a distance of 1500 metres.

■ NELSON'S LAST BATTLE ■

THERE WAS REJOICING in the fleet off Cadiz when the *Victory* arrived. Nelson inspired confidence in his captains, his 'band of brothers', and gave them courage. He had told them that their gun crews were better than those of the French and Spanish and that 'no captain could go wrong if he placed his ship alongside that of an enemy'.

ENEMY SAILS IN SIGHT

On 19 October, distant sails were spotted as the enemy fleet left port. Battle was only hours away. Off Cape Trafalgar, a sandy strip of land jutting into the sea, the ships moved very slowly. Nelson placed his ships between the enemy and the safety of Cadiz harbour. The 26 British ships sailed into battle in two columns. Nelson led one line; Admiral Collingwood in the *Royal Sovereign* led the other. The 33 French and Spanish ships formed a sweeping curve.

SIGNAL FOR BATTLE

Nelson ordered a flag signal to be sent to the

EVENTS

1805 By August, Austria, Russia and Sweden join Britain in the war against France. Battle of Trafalgar and death of Nelson (21 October). In the United States, explorers Lewis and Clark reach the Pacific Ocean after crossing the Rocky Mountains (November). Napoleon is still unbeatable on land. His army defeats the Russians and Austrians at the battle of Austerlitz (December).
1806 Funeral of Nelson. Death of William Pitt (January). France defeats Prussia at battle of Jena (October). Napoleon is not finally defeated until the battle of Waterloo in 1815.

▲ Nelson falls to the deck, mortally wounded, as the battle rages around him.

fleet: 'England confides that every man will do his duty'. The signal officer asked to change *confides* to *expects*. He explained that it would need fewer flags to send.

At midday, the battle of Trafalgar began. The two British columns broke through the enemy line. In a general fight, ships moved close to one another, cannon firing.

THE DEATH OF NELSON

As *Victory*'s guns thundered shot into two French ships, Nelson walked on deck with Captain Hardy. The admiral had insisted on wearing his full uniform, with glittering medals. A marksman perched in the mast-top of the French ship *Redoutable* saw him and fired. Nelson, badly wounded by a musket ball, was carried below deck.

Nothing could be done to save him. He died about 4.30pm, knowing that victory was won. His last words were 'Thank God I have done my duty'. Eighteen enemy ships were captured or destroyed. Admiral Villeneuve himself was taken prisoner.

A HERO'S FUNERAL

The badly damaged *Victory* was towed into Gibraltar. When news of Trafalgar reached London, people wanted to cheer a victory, but instead mourned the death of their brave admiral.

Nelson's body came home in a barrel filled with alcohol. On a cold, clear day in January 1806, his funeral procession moved slowly through London's streets from the River Thames at Whitehall to St Paul's Cathedral. Vast crowds lined the streets to watch in silence. The 'great and gallant Nelson' as *The Times* newspaper called him, had the hero's funeral he had wanted.

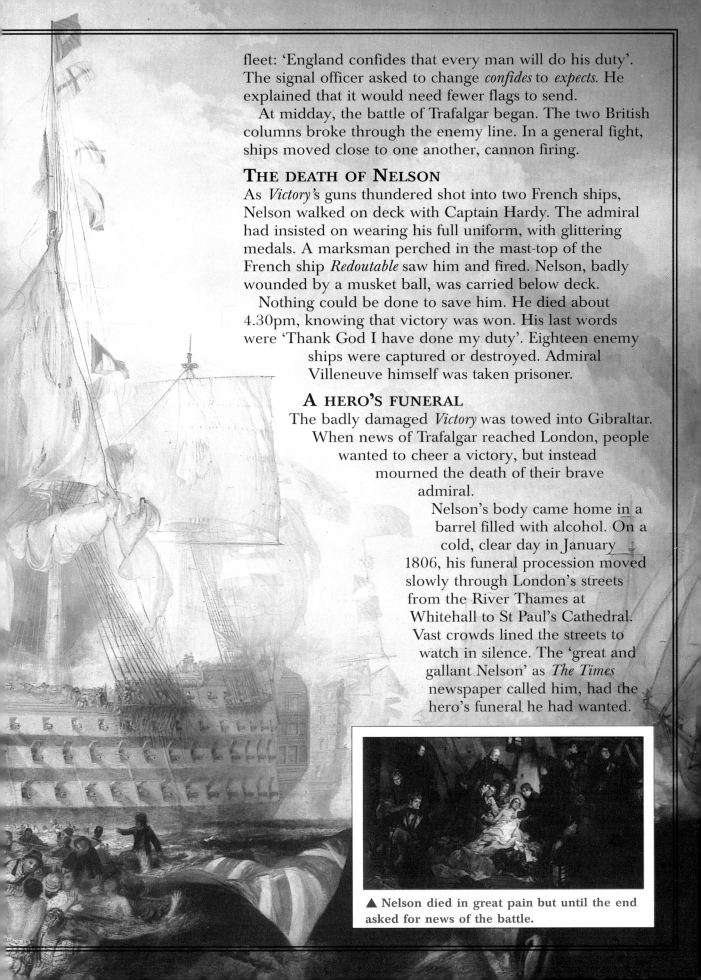

▲ Nelson died in great pain but until the end asked for news of the battle.

■ NELSON'S LEGACY ■

TRAFALGAR SAVED Britain from invasion. The British navy ruled the oceans and did so throughout the 19th century. Nelson's death in victory was seen as a national tragedy. More than ever, he was a British hero. Poems and songs were written about him, his picture was seen on plates, mugs, tea trays, and many other articles. There were posters of him in the streets, paintings of his ships and battles, and a wax figure in Westminster Abbey. Streets, public houses, ships, and even towns were named after him.

Nelson's statue stands in Trafalgar Square on top of Nelson's Column – London's best-known monument. The *Victory* is kept by the Royal Navy in dry dock at Portsmouth.

NELSON'S NAVY

Not long after Trafalgar, steamships began to replace sailing ships like the *Victory*, but the 'Nelson touch' is still an ideal honoured in the Royal Navy. Nelson's shipmates admired his courage and determination. They also loved him for his kindness to young sailors nervous of climbing the mast for the first time, or to 'powder monkeys' – lads working as gunners' mates in the smoke and heat of the gun decks.

Nelson had faults: he was vain, stubborn and unkind to his wife. But the sailors who tore shreds off his funeral flag as keepsakes remembered an admiral who treated

▲ HMS *Victory* is an historic tourist attraction. Visitors can learn about its great admiral and feel for themselves what life was like for sailors who served on the ship.

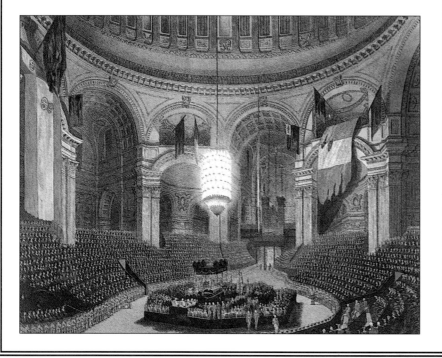

◀ Nelson's coffin lies in state beneath the great dome of St Paul's Cathedral, London, where his state funeral and burial took place.

▶ Nelson's statue on top of its column in Trafalgar Square, London – the best known of all Nelson's monuments. The column was completed in 1843 and is 50 metres high.

them fairly. He set a standard for later sailors of all nations to follow and his battles are still studied in naval colleges.

WHAT HAPPENED TO . . . ?

A grateful nation did not take care of Lady Hamilton, as Nelson had asked. She lost her home and money, and fled to France where she died penniless in 1815. Lady Nelson died in 1831. Nelson's daughter Horatia married a clergyman and died in 1881.

Several of Nelson's captains rose to senior rank in the Royal Navy. Captain Hardy became First Sea Lord and governor of the Greenwich Hospital for old sailors, where Nelson's servant Tom Allen ended his days in 1834.

▼ A mother shows her son 'England's pride and glory'. The poet Robert Southey wrote of Nelson: 'England has had many heroes. But never one who so entirely possessed the love of his fellow countrymen'.

■ GLOSSARY ■

ADMIRAL An officer who holds the highest rank in the navy.

AMBASSADOR A country's most senior official representative in a foreign country.

AMPUTATION Cutting off all or part of a damaged limb or body part.

BARON A title held by a member of the lowest rank of the nobility.

BATTLESHIP The largest kind of heavily armoured warship.

BROADSIDE Either side of a ship, along which cannon were ranged on the decks.

CABIN A room on a ship; in Nelson's day only officers had their own cabins.

CANNON A large, heavy gun that fired solid metal balls.

CAPSTAN A revolving post used to pull in a rope or anchor cable that winds round the capstan as it turns.

CLERGYMAN A minister or priest in the Christian church.

COACH A four-wheeled, horse-drawn carriage.

COLONIST A settler who lives in a colony (an overseas land ruled by the colonist's home country).

COMMAND Having control of something, such as a ship.

COMMANDER-IN-CHIEF A senior military officer in control of a country's armies or naval vessels.

CONVOY A group of ships travelling together or under escort for safety.

CUTLASS A short sword with one cutting edge used by sailors in Nelson's time.

DOCKYARD A place with workshops and equipment for building and repairing ships.

DRUMMER BOY A boy soldier or sailor who beat a drum to call crew or send signals.

ESCORT A companion; in wartime, a warship accompanying merchant ships to guide and protect them.

FIRST SEA LORD In Britain, the senior commander in the Royal Navy.

FLEET A number of warships acting together or a division of the navy under one commander or admiral.

FORT A strong building that can be defended against enemy attack.

FRIGATE A fast sailing-vessel with only one deck of guns. Frigates were used as convoy escorts and scouts for a fleet.

GALLEY The kitchen of a ship.

GOVERNOR The ruler of a colony; in a British colony, the monarch's representative.

GUNNER An experienced seaman whose job it was to train gun crews and to look after the gunpowder and cannonballs.

HAMMOCK A length of canvas or net hung by each end and used as a bed aboard ship.

HOUSE OF LORDS The upper house (assembly) in Britain's parliament. It is made up of unelected nobles, judges and bishops. The lower house is the House of Commons, whose members are elected.

INDUSTRIAL REVOLUTION Important change during the 18th and 19th centuries when industries in Britain became mechanised and factory towns grew quickly.

LIEUTENANT A junior naval officer.

MANSERVANT A male servant, usually someone's personal servant.

MERCHANT SHIP A ship that carries goods; a trading ship.

MIDSHIPMAN Formerly the title of the lowest-ranking officer in the navy.

MISSION A soldier or sailor's task; being sent out to do a particular duty.

MUSKET A rifle-like gun loaded through the muzzle and fired from the shoulder.

MUTINY A revolt or uprising against authority in the army or navy.

NAVY OFFICE The government department that in Nelson's day looked after the day-to-day running of the navy.

OPIUM A pain-relieving drug obtained from the opium poppy.

ORDER OF THE BATH An English order or rank of knighthood.

PARSON A parish priest (clergyman) in the Church of England.

PIOUS Religious.

PLANTATION An estate in tropical countries where crops such as bananas, rubber or cotton are grown on a large scale.

POWDER MONKEY A boy who carried gunpowder to sailors firing guns on a warship.

PRESS GANG Group of sailors sent to seize men for service in the navy.

PRIME MINISTER The leader of parliamentary government in Britain and chief minister.

REAR-ADMIRAL An admiral lower in rank than a vice-admiral, originally in command of the rear ships of a fleet.

RECRUIT A sailor who has newly enlisted (joined the navy) or joined a ship.

RECTORY The house where a rector (clergyman) lives.

REVEREND A title of respect given to a clergyman.

SCURVY A disease caused by a lack of vitamin C (found in fruit and vegetables); symptoms are bleeding gums and pain in the joints.

SHIP OF THE LINE A warship large enough to take its place in a line of battle.

SHIP'S BISCUIT A hard, tasteless biscuit (known also as hardtack) eaten by sailors aboard ship.

SHOT Metal balls or pellets fired from a cannon or gun.

SLOOP A single-masted sailing ship.

SPINNING JENNY An early spinning machine (1764) that enabled several threads to be spun at once.

STAGECOACH A horse-drawn coach that carried passengers and mail from one stage to another along a regular route.

TOPMAN A sailor working on the topsails, at the top of the masts.

TRUCE An agreement between enemies to stop fighting, usually temporarily.

VICE-ADMIRAL A senior naval officer, next in rank to an admiral.

WARSHIP A ship with guns for use in sea battles.

WEEVIL A beetle that damages fruit, nuts and grain, and eats food stores.

YELLOW FEVER A tropical disease that causes jaundice (yellowing of the skin).

VICE-ADMIRAL A senior naval officer.

PLACES TO VISIT

Burnham Thorpe,
Norfolk

Chatham Historic Dockyard,
Chatham, Kent

Maritime Museum,
Bucklers Hard, Beaulieu, Hants

Maritime Museum for East Anglia
Marine Parade, Great Yarmouth, Norfolk

National Maritime Museum,
Greenwich, London

Nelson Museum,
Priory Street, Monmouth

Royal Naval Museum and Victory Gallery,
HM Naval Base, Portsmouth

St Paul's Cathedral,
London

HMS Victory,
HM Naval Base, Portsmouth, Hants

■ INDEX ■

of individuals—why men and women adopt particular roles in families, occupations, and so forth—tend to examine the social psychological processes involved in socialization and social interactions. Although such a focus remains important, it is only a partial explanation of gender. The newer concept of "gendered organizations" allows us to see how gender relations are perpetuated through organizational practices, as well as through socialization and everyday social interaction (see Reskin and Padavic 1994).

For a good understanding of gender, then, we need to look at large-scale processes of organizational change as well as small-scale inter- actions. We also need to consider widespread cultural assumptions that are embedded in our institutions, rather than only individual attitudes and behaviors. People who set policies within workplaces and other organizational settings make many gendered assumptions. For example, the long hours typically required of corporate executives are based on the model of a male worker with a wife who stays at home and takes care of the children and household maintenance. These expectations create hardships for both men and women who want to be involved parents, but they have been particularly damaging to women's careers.

In her study of working parents, *The Second Shift*, Arlie Hochschild describes a woman she calls Ann Myerson, who made it to the top of the corporate world as a well-paid vice president of a large company. However, the demands of Myerson's job, and the fact that she did more of the household work than her husband (the "second shift"), made it extremely difficult for her to spend enough time with her young children. She ended up quitting her job, but she did not tell her employer why she was doing so. As she explained:

> I would lose every shred of credibility with my male colleagues if I told them I needed time with my children. In their world, needing time with children doesn't count as a "real" reason for any decision about your job. So I told them my husband got a more lucrative offer in Boston. They understood that. (Hochschild 1989:98)

Myerson did not feel she could even talk about her needs as a parent in her work environment, much less restructure the corporation to accommodate family needs, and so she quit her job. She chose the gender role of stay-at-home mother, but her choice was influenced less by her socialization as a female than by an organizational structure that made gendered assumptions about its workers.

Fathers, similarly, may work long hours at the expense of involvement with their children not simply because of their male socialization but because they understand that they would be jeopardizing their careers by taking time to care for children. In a study of men's choices regarding work and family commitments, sociologist Kathleen Gerson (1993) explains that it is very difficult for fathers who wish to be involved parents to take time off work because they get the message from their employers that when it comes to taking leaves, "illness is unavoidable, but parenting is voluntary—an indication of lack of job commitment" (pp. 247–48). When asked if he would take a parental leave, one father told Gerson:

> I'd say yes, but realistically no. It would be a problem because it's very difficult for me to tell my boss that I have to leave at such a time. I have deadlines to meet. If I leave the office for two or three months, my job is in jeopardy. (Gerson 1993:248)

In Sweden, paternity leaves have been available to men for some time, but only a small percentage of eligible fathers take advantage of the benefit (Furstenberg 1988). Men who take paternity leaves put themselves at a disadvantage in competing with others who put in long hours and uninterrupted years of service in accordance with the gendered rhythms of the workplace.

Gender Change and Social Movements

Despite obstacles such as the gendered assumptions of organizations, gender relations have changed. We can begin to explain how changes occur and why inequality between men and women—and conflict over gender—persists by looking at how social movements are related to gender arrangements. *Social movements* are sustained attempts by people with common goals and bonds of solidarity to bring about change through collective action targeted at government authorities or other opponents (see Tarrow 1994:3–6). Participants in social movements take part in various types of actions, ranging from demonstrations to legislative lobbying to symbolic actions such as wearing an armband in protest. They are united by common values or interests, and they share a common identity or basis for solidarity such as living in the same community or belonging to the same ethnic group. The actions of a social movement differ from isolated episodes of collective action, such as a single riot or demonstration, in that they endure for some length of time, typically a number of years, and consist of many challenging acts.

Since the nineteenth century, social movements have become an increasingly common means of bringing about change (see Tilly 1984, 1995). In our time, numerous influential social movements have arisen, including the American civil rights movement, the women's movement, the gay and lesbian rights movement, the environmental movement, and the peace movement. How, then, are these social movements connected to changes in gender? As we will see in subsequent chapters, large-scale social changes that transform gender arrangements also facilitate the emergence of social movements. Social movements, in turn, foster additional transformations in gender relations.

Social Change and the Emergence of Social Movements

To understand how large-scale changes in gender relations affect social movements, first consider how movements in general emerge. We tend to think of social movements as occurring when people are upset about some injustice and decide to do something about it. Indeed, most movements are based on feelings of outrage about injustice. Yet there are many more injustices in the world than there are social movements, and many injustices addressed by movements, such as racism and sexism, had existed for many years before people organized to do something about them. Why do social movements mobilize at particular times to address some issues and not others? Large-scale socioeconomic and political conditions are important to the emergence of social movements, and they set bounds on the changes that movements can bring about.

Social movements emerge when the resources and networks needed to organize are available and when opportunities exist to bring about change. The concept of a "political opportunity structure," used by social movement theorists, captures the idea that certain aspects of the political environment encourage or inhibit collective action. For example, sustained protest is unlikely to occur in societies with highly repressive governments because the costs of dissent are too high and the likelihood of success too low. In addition to the importance of the political environment, social movement theorists have also stressed the effects of the broader cultural and social context (see Rucht 1996). For example, the values promoted by social movements may be more or less consonant with the values of existing social groups and thus influence social support for the movement.

The case of the American civil rights movement illustrates the importance of social and political context. African Americans had long been oppressed in the United States, and in the Southern states they suffered from legal segregation and discrimination. Blacks could not eat at certain restaurants, they had to use "colored" rest room facilities and drinking fountains, they had to sit in the back of buses—or stand when Whites needed their seats—and they were denied basic political rights, including the right to vote, through terrorism employed by the southern Whites who held power. Despite these long-standing grievances, it was not until the 1950s that an effective civil rights movement was organized.

To understand the timing of the civil rights movement, we also need to look at the impact of large-scale social changes (see McAdam 1982; Morris 1984). The decline of cotton as a cash crop in the United States led many southern Blacks to migrate to the cities. With increased urbanization, Black communities grew and supported larger Black churches, which were cultural centers for Black communities. Ministers of urban Black churches could then be supported completely by the Black community and become independent of the dominant White power structure. When the southern civil rights movement got under way, Black churches were central to its organization. Although African Americans had long suffered the indignities and violence that motivated their collective action, these large-scale developments gave them the resources, organizational bases, and leadership necessary to sustain a successful social movement.

At the same time that structural changes can facilitate the mobilization of a social movement, the ability of the movement to bring about change is also limited by structural considerations. The civil rights movement was successful in challenging the segregation of public facilities in the South and in winning voting rights legislation for Blacks in part because the Black vote was highly attractive to the Democratic Party. The movement was able to exploit divisions between northern and southern politicians and divisions in the South between business leaders, who were hurt by economic boycotts, and political leaders, who wanted to maintain segregation. But when the movement turned to economic issues and tried to address the poverty of urban Blacks and other groups, the situation was different. Business and political elites were united in their support for established economic structures, so civil rights leaders had a very difficult time attacking problems such as unemployment and poor housing through direct action tactics. The civil rights movement made few gains when it turned to problems rooted in the economic structure of American society.

Large-scale social changes have also been important to the emergence of gender-based movements, and structural considerations similarly place limitations on changes in gender relations. Because gender relations are central to the political and cultural organization of societies, these arrangements provide both the motivation and the organizational networks for many social movements (Taylor 1996:166–70). Once movements mobilize in the context of particular gender arrangements, they reflect their political and cultural origins in their organizational styles, rhetoric, and strategies (pp. 170–76). For example, the self-help movement that formed in the 1980s to support women suffering from postpartum depression draws on cultural understandings of what it means to be a "good mother" in describing the problem of postpartum depression at the same time that it challenges prevailing ideas about mothering. Support groups formed within the self-help movement are based on the assumption of "traditional feminine responsibility for caring" (Taylor 1996:123).

As Chapter 2 shows, important social changes created the basis for feminist mobilization in the nineteenth and twentieth centuries. Women's movements emerged in at least 32 different countries in the period from the mid-nineteenth to mid-twentieth centuries, and the size of the movements was related to the extent of urbanization and industrialization in the countries where the movements occurred (Chafetz and Dworkin 1986). The two types of changes can easily be linked. With urbanization and industrialization, rates of education increase and a middle class typically emerges. Thus, in the late 1800s and early 1900s, sizable numbers of educated, middle-class women were available for voluntary work in clubs, reform organizations, and social movements, such as the abolition and temperance movements. The ingredients for a women's movement coalesced as women experienced barriers based on gender, which created grievances. At the same time, they gained organizing skills and built networks through their participation in clubs and other civic groups.

In most cases, however, women's movements of the nineteenth and early twentieth centuries did not advocate fundamental changes in gender roles. Instead, they accepted the traditional idea of separate spheres for men and women and sought the means for women to perform their traditional roles more effectively. For example, many women's suffragists saw the vote as a way for women to exert their moral authority in the public sphere, not as a way to advance equality between men and women. This limited view of the changes possible in gender roles was imposed by the structure of society; women's roles had not yet expanded enough to permit more radical ideas to spread among significant numbers of women (Chafetz and Dworkin 1986). In some countries, such as the United States, small numbers of feminists advocated more radical ideas about gender, but they did not attract large followings, and their equal-rights arguments gave way to more traditional justifications for change (Buechler 1986; Chafetz and Dworkin 1986). In the second half of the twentieth century, after large numbers of women had entered the labor force, women's consciousness changed, and women's movements in numerous countries began to advocate more fundamental changes in gender relations. Thus, structural changes are important in producing shifts in gender roles, such as women's increased participation in the public arena, that then facilitate the emergence of social movements. At the same time, structural conditions limit the change that movements can achieve.

The Effects of Social Movements on Gender Relations

An explicit aim of women's movements and the recent men's movements (see Kimmel 1989) is change in gender relations, but other movements have also affected gender arrangements. Intentionally or not, social movements may alter men's and women's roles, expand the consciousness of movement participants and the public at large, introduce new organizational strategies and means of expression (see Taylor 1996:172–76), and create new cultural practices and discourse on new topics.

Women who participated in the civil rights movement, for example, experienced the joy of learning new skills and acting effectively in the public arena. As a result, they changed their ideas about what women can do. Bernice Reagon, a member of the Student Nonviolent Coordinating Committee (SNCC), described her participation in the civil rights group in such terms:

> One of the things that happened to me through SNCC was my whole world expanded in what I could do as a person. . . . I think if you talked to a lot of people who participated in the movement, who were in SNCC, you find women describing themselves being pushed in ways they had never experienced before. (Quoted in Robnett 1996:1676)

Women who worked in both the civil rights and antiwar movements in the 1960s began to think not only about race relations and governmental power but also about gender. As a result, they helped to organize the women's movement (Evans 1979).

Similarly, some men responded to the women's movement by reconsidering their own roles. A men's liberation movement formed in the early 1970s to critique the "male sex role," arguing that it often resulted in unfulfilling work, unhappy marriages, unsatisfactory relationships with children, and a lack of close friends (Kimmel 1996:280). Although the men's liberation movement reached only a very small number of

American men, it was part of a broader cultural shift in ideas about masculinity (p. 286). Television shows in the 1970s no longer featured wise patriarchs, as they had in the 1950s and early 1960s, but instead presented men like Archie Bunker, who were typically "the butt of humor, not the object of veneration" (Kimmel 1996:290).

Related to changes in consciousness about gender are shifts in cultural practices. The ways people talk about gender issues play an important part in determining how gender-related policies develop. For example, in France, where women were not granted the vote until 1944, public discussion of women's suffrage was limited by the "universe of political discourse" (Jenson 1987). Key political actors, including social movements and political parties, hewed to the dominant view that women were important as members of families and not as individuals. Thus, women's suffrage was not discussed as a means of creating equality between men and women. Rather, advocates saw women's suffrage as a way to bring the nurturing influence of mothers to the political arena; as voters, women would support policies that benefited children and families. One of the key influences on this discourse was a "family movement" that became active after World War I to encourage large families. It was not until the emergence of the modern women's movement in France in the late 1960s that new ways of talking about women entered the public discourse and themes such as women's right to control their bodies and women's equality were employed in policy debates over abortion and other issues (Jenson 1987:82).

The new ways of talking that are created by social movements are also used by individuals in their everyday lives. For example, political scientist Jane Mansbridge (1993) talked to some lower-class Black and White women and found that they used some feminist terms such as "male chauvinist" as they struggled through their relationships with men. These women had never been active in the women's movement and would not call themselves feminists, but they had adopted certain basic feminist tenets, like the idea that male domination is unjust (Mansbridge 1993:27). Gender change is also evident in now common practices, such as the use of male and female pronouns where male pronouns were once used exclusively. And whereas married women once lost their identities completely in formal titles such as "Mrs. John Smith," English-speaking women now have the option of using the title "Ms.," which, like "Mr.," does not reveal marital status. Women may also choose to keep their own surnames after marriage, following the precedent of nineteenth-century American feminist Lucy Stone. These and other cultural changes, such as changes in dress, are directly related to social movement activity.

By raising consciousness and introducing new ways of talking about gender, social movements help to provide the vision, as well as the organization and tactics, needed to bring about cultural and policy changes. But social movements also generate conflicts over gender. Full-fledged *countermovements* may emerge to oppose the initiatives of an existing movement. In the 1970s, the countermovement against the Equal Rights Amendment (ERA) was instrumental in its defeat despite solid public support for the ERA (see Chapter 4). The anti-abortion movement formed as a countermovement to the abortion rights movement, resulting in a prolonged conflict over legal abortion (see Chapter 5). Such battles between opposing movements often limit changes in gender relations.

Yet movements do have an impact on gender. In popular culture, we have seen movement-inspired changes in male and female dress, language, and sports, and in media depictions of men and women. In politics, we have seen shifts in party participation and voting and changes in public discourse regarding gender. Within organized religion, churches and synagogues have been forced to make changes related to gender, and outside the mainstream, new male and female spirituality movements have arisen. In the military, women have taken up new roles, and both men and women have been forced to deal with issues such as sexual harassment. Within universities, feminists have pushed for women's studies departments and women's affairs offices that advocate changes in gender relations.

A Look Ahead

In industrialized Western countries, men and women have traditionally performed distinct gender roles. The family has been women's sphere; men have dominated the public arenas of politics, culture, and business. Women have been responsible for raising children and creating a nurturing home; men have provided financially for their families. Even when women have acted in public venues, they have frequently done much of the "emotion work" of society, particularly by acting in ways that make others feel more comfortable and secure (Hochschild 1983:165). But much has changed in recent decades. This book is concerned with the ways in which social movements have helped women to enlarge their sphere beyond the roles of wife, mother, and nurturer, and it is also concerned with how men have been changing in response.

I do not attempt to cover all the numerous areas of gender change related to social movement activity. Instead, as the title of the book suggests, I focus on changes related to gender roles in the family and the gendered organizations related to family life. I stress the role of social movements in creating change within political and cultural contexts. That is, I examine movements as sources of change in gender, and I also explore the forces that resist change and the conflicts that occur over gender issues.

Chapter 2 lays out some of the large-scale social changes related to gender and family that have occurred in the nineteenth and twentieth centuries, such as industrialization and urbanization. Chapter 3 examines the role of six particular social movements in creating feminist consciousness in the context of the larger social changes described in Chapter 2: the temperance, abolition, and civil rights movements, the New Left, Women's Strike for Peace, and the environmental movement. Some of these movements built on existing gender relations and emphasized women's differences from men; others tried to create a new consciousness of men's and women's equality. Chapter 4 looks at some attempts to translate feminist consciousness into social policies intended to create equal rights and opportunities for women. It describes how the Equal Rights Amendment generated controversy in the United States over fundamental shifts in men's and women's traditional spheres. Similarly, Chapters 5 and 6 examine how two issues, abortion and homosexuality, have generated intense conflict in part because they symbolize fundamental changes in gender and family relations. Chapter 7 concludes by assessing the changes brought about by social movements, the reasons for conflict over gender and family issues, and the prospects for further change in gender relations.

2

Gender, Family, and Social Change

Men and women have long held separate and unequal positions in many different societies, yet they have not always recognized or questioned the unfairness of gender relations. In industrialized Western societies, women conventionally have been expected to care for the home, make the coffee at work, and in general put the needs of men and children ahead of their own. Men have been expected to earn a living, outshine women in social status, and act as authority figures in the home.

These gender restrictions are longstanding because many forces operate to maintain them. Gender relations are institutionalized in organizational patterns such as work schedules that leave little time for family life. Cultural conceptions of the "good mother" and the "good provider" (Bernard 1981) are widely shared. Even our language is filled with assumptions about gender.

Nevertheless, changes in gender relations are occurring. Large-scale social changes in the nineteenth and twentieth centuries, which are described in this chapter, altered men's and women's lives in ways that challenged existing gender arrangements. Some people consequently became more receptive to the messages of social movements seeking deliberately to alter gender and family relations. At the same time, however, widespread social changes also scared some people, who felt that their lifestyles and values were endangered. Thus, some people resisted changes in the family and women's role as homemaker while others promoted new values and gender relations.

During times of rapid change, "the family" has often symbolized social stability and traditional values. In contemporary American political culture, as in earlier times, "family values" are continually invoked by politicians seeking to reassure the public that economic and social problems can be controlled. In reality, however, families have never been the stable and conflict-free sanctuaries that supporters of the "traditional" family imagine (Coontz 1992). In this chapter, we will look at some of the major social changes that have prompted both movements for change and countermovements resisting change in family and gender relations.

The Impact of Industrialization and Urbanization

In the nineteenth century, large-scale social changes that affected men's and women's roles were occurring in a number of Western countries. Industrialization and urbanization created dramatic changes in the ways people lived and worked (see Chafetz and Dworkin 1986). Industrialization separated production from the home and created many new types of jobs. Urbanization brought people into closer contact with one another and allowed access to the new jobs.

Along with these large-scale trends came a number of other important changes: Both men and women began acquiring more formal education as new labor force skills were emphasized and access to schools increased. The middle class grew in size as industrialization created greater wealth. Members of the growing middle class gained more leisure time, which they could devote to voluntary work. Birth rates declined because the large numbers of children who were useful in an agrarian economy became a burden in an industrial economy.

Gender Ideologies and Social Change

As the relative security of an agrarian way of life gave way to the uncertainty of the expanding marketplace, the shape of the typical family began to change. In the "traditional" family of preindustrial times, women and men had distinct roles, but both were engaged in productive agrarian work. Industrialization helped to create what some historians and social scientists (for example, Shorter 1975; Stacey 1990) call the "modern" family: the intact nuclear family consisting of husband as breadwinner, wife as full-time homemaker and mother, and dependent children. (In popular usage today, the "modern" family is typically referred to as "traditional.")

As industrialization took hold, the family took on great symbolic significance, particularly in middle-class culture. Domestic ideologies, emphasizing women's moral virtues and differences from men, arose in a number of Western countries (Koven and Michel 1990:1085). Women were looked to as the source of social values and stability. A "cult of true womanhood" emerged in nineteenth-century America:

> In a society where values changed frequently, where fortunes rose and fell with frightening rapidity, where social and economic mobility provided instability as well as hope, one thing at least remained the same—a true woman was a true woman, wherever she was found. (Welter 1966:151–52)

Men competed in the cutthroat world of business, but the family was a "haven in a heartless world," with women as its keepers (see Lasch 1977).

Nineteenth-century advice books and popular literature portrayed women as naturally pious and virtuous, in contrast to men, who were morally compromised by natural lust and sinfulness. At the same time, women who failed to display the piety, purity, submissiveness, and domesticity that were the "cardinal virtues" of true womanhood were warned of suffering an ugly fate (Welter 1966:152). For example, one popular story told of a young woman who lost her virtue to "the sophistry of a gay, city youth" and ended up dying along with her baby (pp. 155–56). Other stories and advice books warned women against reading morally unacceptable literature, including books that questioned women's place in the home, and of moral failings such as poor housekeeping. In a world that was changing, women became the guardians of public morality.

Large-scale social and economic transformations also brought new ideologies about manhood. Before the expansion of commercialization and industrialization, men had occupied relatively fixed social positions, such as small landowner or craftsman, and did not need to seek their fortunes or forge their identities. Before work became separated from home, the husband was the head of the family enterprise; with the development of capitalism, he became the breadwinner (Skolnick 1991:38). In *Manhood in America*, sociologist Michael Kimmel (1996) shows that the notion of the "self-made man" came into being when men had to prove themselves in the marketplace. In the rising middle class of the nineteenth century, the self-made man achieved his position in the world by hard work and individual initiative. Because his identity was no longer fixed, "his sense of himself as a man was in constant need of demonstration" (Kimmel 1996:43). Men proved themselves in the workplace under the eyes of other men. The self-made man could be found in every European country, but was particularly important in America, "the land of immigrants and democratic ideals, the land without hereditary titles" (p. 17).

By the mid-nineteenth century in America, a cult of the self-made man complemented the cult of true womanhood. Popular biographies and advice books told men that they could get rich if they could only exercise self-control over their passions, including their sexual desires. Boys were warned not to masturbate, and husbands were advised to limit the frequency of their sexual relations to perhaps once a month, so as to preserve their energy for economic endeavors. While middle-class girls were being taught the virtues of true womanhood, boys were being taught to be aggressive, self-reliant, and self-controlled so that they could participate in the competitive world of men's work (Kimmel 1996:55).

Eventually, the "doctrine of separate spheres" became dominant, confining women to the home, while men occupied the work world (Pleck 1993:1950). In mid-nineteenth-century America, married women lacked the right to own property, to enter into legal contracts, or to have legal custody of their children (Giele 1995:52). For men, the home was supposed to be a haven from the heartless world of work, but in reality "men were increasingly exiled from the home" (Kimmel 1996:58). Men became the breadwinners of families, but had less and less time to spend with their wives and children as they worked to be good providers. The worlds of men and women were becoming increasingly separate, for the working class as well as for the middle class—although the working class emphasized male authority more than female virtue (Kimmel 1996:56).

Some men threw themselves into the breadwinner role, but others sought to escape the constraints on their lives, including the efforts of women to civilize them. In America, men who wanted to flee from the demands of self-control could, in the words of Huckleberry Finn, "light out for the territory." The American West was a place where men could go to pursue their ambitions, to escape their failures, and to enjoy the freedom of life among men "outside the conventional boundaries of civilization and away from wives." Thus, one way in which men could be men was to escape from feminine influence. Short of going west, men distanced themselves from femininity by, for example, wearing the beards and mustaches that became popular in the 1840s and 1850s (Kimmel 1996:59–62).

Although the cults of true womanhood and of the self-made man helped to order a changing world for nineteenth-century men and women, these gender ideologies never matched the realities of people's lives. While women were depicted as domestic stabilizers and men as achieving breadwinners, women were in fact changing along with men, both through increased labor force participation and reform work in the public arena.

Women's Labor Force Participation

By 1900, one-fifth of American women were in the labor force (Wertheimer 1977:210). Many middle- and upper-class White women were not satisfied with the domestic role they had been assigned. However, few professions other than teaching and nursing were open to them in the nineteenth and early twentieth centuries, and these paid poorly and typically required women to be unmarried (Wertheimer 1977:243). Women who went to college were faced with the problem of what to do after finishing their degrees. Jane Addams, who graduated from Rockford Seminary in 1881, spent seven years trying to find a suitable career and finally helped to found the settlement house movement (Ware 1989:41–42). Many middle-class women in the industrializing world took up voluntary activities.

Poor and working-class women had a notably different experience when they began to enter the labor force. Like their middle-class counterparts, they were confined to a very narrow range of paid employment in industrial economies in the nineteenth and early twentieth centuries (Chafetz and Dworkin 1986:72–73). But their prospects were even less attractive. Poor African-American women typically worked either as agricultural workers, laundry workers, or domestic servants. Writing in 1912, an anonymous Black woman described working 14- to 16-hour days as a domestic servant, being compelled to live in her employer's home, and being permitted to visit her own children only once every two weeks. As she put it, "You might as well say that I'm on duty all the time—from sunrise to sunrise, every day in the week. I am the slave, body and soul, of this family" (Ware 1989:72–73).

White working-class women who found jobs in factories in America's expanding industrial economy also had hard lives. They worked at "women's jobs" in textile mills, tobacco factories, laundries, shoe factories, food processing and canning plants, and other industries. These were mostly unskilled jobs that involved grueling labor under exploitive conditions, offered no chance of advancement, and paid a fraction of what men earned (Wertheimer 1977:210). For example, Agnes Nestor worked in a glove factory where workers were paid by the piece and had to pay "machine rent" for the sewing machines they used, in addition to buying their own needles and machine oil (Ware 1989:81). As Nestor wrote in 1898, the system

> encourages a girl to do more than her physical strength will allow her to do continuously. . . . When I started in the trade and saw the girls working at that dreadful pace every minute, I wondered how they could keep up the speed. (Quoted in Ware 1989:85)

Helen Campbell, in her 1893 book *Women Wage-Earners*, described similarly exploitive conditions in other jobs:

> Feather-sorters, fur-workers, cotton-sorters, all workers on any material that gives off dust, are subject to lung and bronchial troubles. In soap factories the girls' hands are eaten by the caustic soda, and by the end of the day the fingers are often raw and bleeding. In making buttons, pins, and other manufactures . . . there is always liability of getting the fingers

jammed or caught. For the first three times the wounds are dressed without charge. After that the injured person must pay expenses. (Quoted in Wertheimer 1977:213)

As the economy expanded, office jobs and sales jobs also became available to women. These white-collar jobs were considered more desirable than factory jobs because they were cleaner and safer. As a result, they typically went to the daughters of native-born Americans, while industrial jobs went to the daughters of immigrants. However, all women's wages were low and the work was always hard. For example, switchboard operators took 250 to 350 calls per hour, and saleswomen stood for 12 or more hours a day (Wertheimer 1977:237–39).

Most of the women who entered the labor force in the nineteenth century were young and single. Because it was increasingly difficult to combine child care and productive labor in an industrial economy, married women with children tended to work outside the home only when their monetary contributions to the family were essential (Tilly and Scott 1978). Children worked to supplement the family income when necessary. Because they were concentrated in low-paying female jobs with long hours and harsh working conditions, young women looked forward to getting married and quitting work. Some urban women also turned to prostitution, which paid five times more than the typical female wage (Ware 1989:66–67).

To improve their working conditions, working-class women such as Agnes Nestor became involved in union organizing. Despite some successful female strikes and organizing drives, however, the male-dominated unions in the United States were typically uninterested in organizing female workers. They argued that the women would quit work when they married and that the goal of unions should be a "family wage" for men so that they could support their families as breadwinners. As an alternative to unionization, reformers pushed for protective labor legislation, such as limited working hours for women (Ware 1989:67). Many middle-class women, such as those in the settlement house movement, became involved in working to alleviate the problems of working women.

Middle-Class Reformers

Middle-class reform movements were one important response to the changes associated with industrialization and urbanization. Women who were looking for outlets for their talents were particularly important to many movements such as the temperance movement, as we will see in Chapter 3. Middle-class women began to expand their activities outside the home by participating in activities such as organized religion, which were considered socially acceptable because they were compatible with women's domestic role. More women—especially White middle- and upper-class women—also pursued education as one of the duties of "Republican Motherhood" (Kerber 1980). To educate their own children and to serve as teachers in the schools, women themselves had to be educated. Although the early schools for women emphasized moral and domestic training, some seminaries and colleges also offered genuine academic training for women (see Flexner 1959).

Education was critical to the expansion of women's roles beyond the home. The idea that woman's place was in the home persisted, but new ideas about women's roles in society also emerged among women educators and students. The aspirations of many women were raised through education, and their experiences were greatly expanded. One important result was that, as middle-class women came into contact with one another and formed strong friendships, they developed new social networks that carried over into reform work (see Cott 1978; Dubois 1978; Smith-Rosenberg 1975).

Because there were few professions open to women once they completed their schooling and because they had fewer children than ever before, many women became involved in religion, charitable work, and moral reform movements. Women were central to the activist religions, including evangelicalism, that spread through a number of Western countries in the nineteenth century (Koven and Michel 1990:1085). Quakerism, which began in Great Britain and spread to the American colonies, was particularly attractive to women because of its traditions of holding women's business meetings, allowing women to become ministers, and encouraging women to speak out on issues of moral concern (Chafetz and Dworkin 1986:13–14; Giele 1995:32–33). Not surprisingly, many of the American women's rights leaders in the nineteenth century were Quakers. Through Quakerism and other religions dominated by women, White middle-class women began to participate in a community outside the home.

Through religious and charitable work, women developed a moral vision of community life. In this realm, women were the moral equals, if not superiors, of men, and they found satisfaction in living out their ideals through their work. For example, women became heavily involved in home and foreign missions and were inspired by the examples of missionary couples in which women served along with their husbands "as living examples of Christian life" and as models of relatively equal marital relationships (Giele 1995:40). Through women's benevolent associations, middle-class women tried to assist poor women and children, extending their nurturing role outside the home to the community.

Social problems associated with city life were of particular concern to reformers, both male and female, in the nineteenth and early twentieth centuries. With industrialization, people were no longer tied to the land and the local community and moved about in search of jobs. Urban areas offered new attractions such as dance halls and theaters, new freedoms in areas such as mate selection and sexuality, and new dangers such as illegitimate births and prostitution. In cities such as New York, an "urban bachelor subculture" developed in furnished room and tenement districts, making possible new lifestyles outside of the nuclear family, including a gay male subculture (Chauncey 1994). Young women who held jobs "marked out a cultural terrain distinct from familial traditions and the customary practices of their ethnic groups" as they adopted new fashions and hairstyles and tried cosmetics and cigarettes (Peiss 1986:47–48). In response to these perceived threats to family life and to the dangers of working-class culture, middle-class reformers began organizing anti-vice and social-purity societies in the 1870s. Although White middle-class women had the most time and resources for reform work, working-class women also participated in women's organizations, as well as in unions. African-American women became heavily involved in their own clubs and churches, focusing on racial issues and other social welfare concerns (Isenberg 1993).

Female reformers were particularly concerned with the problems of women and with men's abuse of women. They formed moral reform societies to fight prostitution and other forms of exploitation. "Maternalist" movements—based on "ideologies that exalted women's capacity to mother and extended to society as a whole the values of care, nurturance, and morality"—spread in many Western countries (Koven and Michel 1990:1079). In these efforts, women often tried to reform men, sometimes trying to coerce them into acting morally. For example, in 1837 an American reform newspaper called the *Advocate of Moral Reform* published the names of men who engaged prostitutes. Through such moral reform activities, women challenged the behavior of men and developed "feelings of sisterhood as they identified with one another as women" (Giele 1995:44).

Twentieth-Century Social Changes

As the twentieth century progressed, significant demographic changes in the family occurred that further altered gender and family arrangements. The birth rate declined throughout the Western world; the postwar baby boom that occurred in America between 1946 and 1964 was an anomaly in the trend toward increasingly lower birth rates in the twentieth century (see Figure 2.1). The divorce rate also began to climb, rising sharply in the 1960s and, in the United States, leveling off at a very high rate in the 1980s (see Figure 2.2). The age of both men and women at their first marriage began to rise in the 1960s, returning to patterns that had existed earlier in the century. Longevity had been increasing for many decades throughout the industrialized world.

What these trends meant was that women were spending fewer years of their lives raising children and being married to men who were supporting them financially; they had both time and reason to pursue work outside the home. Men, for their part, enjoyed more years without family responsibilities and found their role as family provider declining (see Bernard 1981; Ehrenreich 1983).

Gender and Work

These demographic changes were accompanied by important economic shifts that affected employment and work experiences. By the turn of the century in America, businesses were becoming bigger, and fewer and fewer men owned their own shops or farms. Technological advances led to a decline in skilled work, and managers typically attempted to standardize work performance. Under these conditions, it was hard to exercise the manly virtues of autonomy and self-control in the workplace. Moreover, immigrants, Blacks, and women were joining the labor force in greater numbers, increasing White men's anxieties. And there was no longer a frontier to which men could escape (Kimmel 1996:83–87).

Throughout the twentieth century, as the number of employed women rose, they too experienced important changes in the patterns of their work. Women increasingly worked throughout their lives rather than only before marriage. Beginning with World War II, married women over the age of 35 began to work outside the home in large numbers, and by the 1980s, a majority of married women with young children had joined the labor force. In addition to joining the labor force, women were gaining higher education in record numbers. In the United States in 1960,

FIGURE 2.1

Total Fertility Rates, 1940–1990

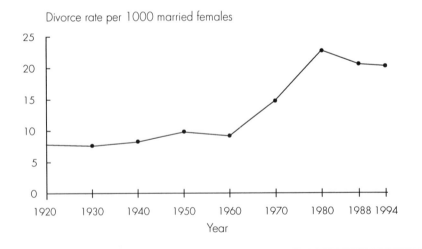

Expected Number of Lifetime Births per Woman

Sources: Statistical Abstract of the United States (1995); Historical Statistics of the United States (1989).

FIGURE 2.2

Divorce Rates, 1920–1994

Divorce rate per 1000 married females

Source: Monthly Vital Statistics Report (1995); Datapedia of the United States (1994).

women earned about a third of all bachelor's degrees awarded; by the 1990s, they were earning over 50 percent of all bachelor's degrees (see Costello and Stone 1994:275).

Increases in women's employment did not automatically lead to greater equality in the workplace or to changes in public attitudes regarding men's and women's family roles (Chafe 1991). Although women's employment opportunities varied by race and class, all women were discriminated against by employers, unions, and government because they were regarded as marginal and temporary workers. The idea that men were the breadwinners and that women's place was in the home was strongly entrenched. Even during the Depression, when young women were forced to postpone marriage and children and many married women had to help support their families, most men and women in the United States continued to oppose women's work outside the home and favored laws that limited job opportunities for married women. An ongoing women's rights movement did push for an Equal Rights Amendment following the passage of women's suffrage, but the movement remained relatively small until the 1960s (Rupp and Taylor 1987).

It was not until World War II, when women were recruited to the workforce as a patriotic duty, that employment of married women became socially acceptable. However, the war did not produce radical changes in gender arrangements. Throughout the war, women's domestic skills were praised as they assisted the war effort through such volunteer tasks as canning, knitting, and saving fats (May 1988:73). Many women joined the paid labor force, but when they took jobs held previously by men, they were paid less (p. 75). After the war, few were able to retain such jobs and federal support for child-care facilities, which had been inadequate even during the war, ended (Chafe 1991:164–65). Some women who returned to the home after the war were happy to "return to normalcy" and begin delayed families, but others had little choice in the matter. Nevertheless, women's postwar levels of labor force participation remained higher than those of the prewar years and continued to rise.

As in the nineteenth century, when domestic ideologies looked to women and the family for security in a time of rapid change, the family took on added importance as a symbol of stability and traditional values. In the postwar era of the Cold War, the family was seen as a source of national strength (May 1988). Women were asked "to embrace domesticity in service to the nation, in the same spirit that they had come to the country's aid by taking wartime jobs" (p. 102). Some authors warned of the ill effects of family instability and women's work outside the home on children and on women themselves. In her best-selling book, Betty

Friedan (1963) argued that there was a postwar "feminine mystique" that portrayed women as happiest in their roles as mothers and homemakers even though many women were in fact discontent.

Looking back at American public opinion polls of the 1940s, historian William Chafe (1991:167) concludes that after World War II, female employment was tolerated by men and women only to the extent that it did not challenge the man's role as provider or the woman's responsibility to raise her children. Men and women opposed the idea of women taking jobs away from men, but they tolerated work by women with grown children, and they viewed women's economic contributions to families as an asset. Many people feared the decline of "traditional values" that was associated in part with women's employment. They could support women's work, however, if it was seen as an extension of women's role in the home. It was acceptable if the woman was "working to give her children a better life and a healthier environment, not attempting to strike out on her own in the selfish pursuit of personal ambition" (Chafe 1991:168).

In postwar America, women's earnings were essential to the survival of lower-class families, but inflation and expanding consumerism made women's employment increasingly important to middle-class families as well. Women's earnings helped to buy such "extras" as a second car and a college education for both the sons and daughters of middle-class families. Since the 1970s, with the decline of high-paying industrial jobs and other economic shifts, real wages have declined and families have struggled to remain in the middle class, making a second income even more critical.

Ironically, the idea that women could legitimately work to enhance life for their families not only helped to justify their labor force participation, but also helped to impede progress toward equality in the workplace (Chafe 1991:170). Because they were viewed as working for extra paychecks rather than careers, women were relegated to sex-segregated, low-paying jobs. At the same time, there was no social commitment to services such as high-quality child care, which would have helped women pursue careers but would have implied a change in traditional values regarding family.

Nevertheless, the entry of millions of women into the labor force had important long-term consequences: "[A]n important cultural line had been crossed. During the 1950s, the meanings that had been implied by married women's working—lower-class status or a husband in dire financial straits—quietly faded away" (Skolnick 1991:53). Women were not only employed, but many were clearly finding self-fulfillment and enjoying the sense of accomplishment that came with work outside the home.

Men, for their part, also began to adopt new roles. By the early twentieth century, although the husband still acted as a breadwinner, a new ideal of companionate marriage encouraged him to help his wife at home and play with the children (Pleck 1993:1954). It had become more and more difficult for men to prove their masculinity through work and, during the Depression, unemployed men could no longer be breadwinners. Consequently, men looked to other arenas in which they might succeed, including the home. After World War II, when many women accepted domestic identities, many middle-class men also looked to the family as the source of meaning in their lives (May 1988:87).

Family life became attractive to men as a source of "the sense of power they were not likely to experience at work" (May 1988:88). Despite the ideal of the companionate marriage, a majority of both men and women in postwar America believed that men should "wear the pants." Popular writers, who feared the emasculation of boys raised solely by their mothers, encouraged fathers to become involved with their sons. Fathers were considered particularly important as a masculine influence in the increasingly suburban, middle-class world of the 1950s. Thus, men could express their masculinity at home rather than at work. As *Esquire* magazine's *Handbook for Hosts* commented, "When a barbecue goes into operation, it automatically becomes a masculine project. After all, outdoor cooking is a man's job" (quoted in Kimmel 1996:246).

Cultural Images of Gender and Family

After World War II, women continued to derive much of their self-esteem from their roles as homemakers and mothers even while many were working outside the home (Klein 1984:88). Men still gained prestige from their ability to be "good providers," even though this role was declining and they were increasingly expected to be family men as well (Bernard 1981; Skolnick 1991). Contradictory cultural images of gender roles and family life revealed both the changes and resistance to change that characterized men's and women's lives.

One image of women in the media provided evidence to Betty Friedan (1963) of a "feminine mystique." For example, *Look* magazine reported in 1956:

> The American woman is winning the battle of the sexes. Like a teenager, she is growing up and confounding her critics. . . . No longer a psychological immigrant to man's world, she works, rather casually, as a third of the

U.S. labor force, less toward a "big career" than as a way of filling a hope chest or buying a new home freezer. She gracefully concedes the top jobs to men. This wondrous creature also marries younger than ever, bears more babies and looks and acts far more feminine than the "emancipated" girl of the 1920's or even 30's. Steelworker's wife and Junior Leaguer alike do their own housework. . . . Today, if she makes an old-fashioned choice and lovingly tends a garden and a bumper crop of children, she rates louder hosannas than ever before. (Quoted in Friedan 1963:52–53)

In this piece of popular writing from the 1950s, women's domestic role was clearly glorified.

Not all magazine articles in the postwar period presented such a one-dimensional image of women, however. A systematic analysis of popular American magazines in the postwar era shows that "domestic ideals coexisted in ongoing tension with an ethos of individual achievement that celebrated nondomestic activity, individual striving, public service, and public success" (Meyerowitz 1994:231). Many articles talked about the achievements of individual women in careers and public life, portraying a range of options for women. Often, however, women were depicted "both as feminine and domestic and as public achievers." For example, a 1952 article about Dorothy McCullough Lee described her as an "ethereally pale housewife" who had waged a successful campaign against gambling and prostitution as the mayor of Portland, Oregon. Similarly, a 1948 article in *Ebony* magazine described a Black female mechanic at American Airlines and mother of two as "a good cook, but an even better mechanic" (Meyerowitz 1994:232–33).

Popular magazines of the forties and fifties typically did not challenge traditional gender roles explicitly, and they rarely dealt with the real problems that women had in combining domestic and nondomestic roles (Meyerowitz 1994:237). In general, the articles of the period reflected societal ambivalence and tensions regarding gender and family. For example, a 1946 article in *Ladies' Home Journal* applauded the successes of career women, but also questioned whether a married career woman has enough time for her husband and children. An article in *Ebony* quoted one career woman as saying, "I like my life just as it is" and another as warning, "Don't sacrifice marriage for career" (Meyerowitz 1994:239).

Images of women in television shows of the postwar era were also quite mixed, reflecting the societal struggle over gender and family relations (Douglas 1994). Shows such as *I Love Lucy* and *The Honeymooners* featured women as housewives with loud voices and slapstick movements who "refused to be contained in the home or limited by the prevailing orthodoxy about appropriate female comportment" (Douglas

1994:50). By the late 1950s, however, such shows were replaced by others such as *Leave It to Beaver* and *Father Knows Best*, which portrayed "cookie-cutter moms" and fathers as benevolent authority figures (p. 51).

Media images of men were also contradictory. For example, a 1954 issue of *McCall's* magazine focused on the importance of family life and the "togetherness" of men, women, and children. One article praised a paper-mill executive who shared child care and household chores with his wife and even helped decorate the family home. But another article in the same issue warned, "For the sake of every member of the family, the family needs a head. This means Father, not Mother" (quoted in Skolnick 1991:71). Men were urged to take responsibility as husbands and fathers in the home, but they were also warned not to become "feminized." Philip Wylie in a 1958 article in *Playboy* bemoaned the way in which the home had become "a boudoir-kitchen-nursery, dreamed up by women, for women, and as if males did not exist as males" because men had not asserted themselves as men (quoted in Kimmel 1996:255–56).

Some novels and popular writings of the 1950s began to attack middle-class conformity and to lament the restrictions placed on men by family life (Ehrenreich 1983). *Playboy* magazine, which was first published in 1953, promoted the pleasures of being a male consumer without family responsibilities and blamed women for enslaving men. As a contributor to the magazine wrote in 1953, "All woman wants is security. And she's perfectly willing to crush man's adventurous, freedom-loving spirit to get it" (quoted in Ehrenreich 1983:47). The writings of psychiatrists and psychologists further legitimized the "male rebellion," warning that men were suffering from coronary heart disease as a result of the burdens of their restrictive breadwinning role. These medical concerns were quickly taken up by popular magazines, such as *McCall's*, which in 1964 published a story called "Five Husbands Who Might Have Lived" about outstanding breadwinners who had demanding wives and died young (Ehrenreich 1983:77). Thus, the breadwinning role was being challenged, and women were being blamed, well before the women's movement and the antifeminist countermovement began to do battle in the 1970s.

The mass media also spread other types of challenges to traditional ideas about gender and family. In 1960, approval of the birth control pill for use in the United States provoked a great deal of media discussion, as did ideas about overpopulation, which undermined the ideology of motherhood (Klein 1984:89–90). The "sexual revolution" also became big news in the 1960s, and in 1962 Helen Gurley Brown's *Sex and the Single Girl* became a best-seller. Brown's single girl went to great lengths to please men, but "she also opened up new possibilities for women" by having sex before marriage and finding fulfillment in a job (Douglas 1994:68–69).

Youth Culture

Another important twentieth-century change was that peer culture became a highly influential source of socialization for teenagers. Peer groups for boys and girls had also been important in traditional agrarian societies, but they differed from modern peer groups in that they were firmly controlled by the adult community (Shorter 1975). With the growth of cities, however, working-class teenagers began fraternizing at movie theaters, amusement parks, penny arcades, and candy shops, and reformers fretted over how to protect children from urban life (Nasaw 1985).

After World War II, the numbers of Blacks and lower-class youths attending high schools alongside middle-class Whites increased significantly, exposing the latter to new youth cultures (Gilbert 1986:18–19). By the 1950s, the mass media were bringing youth culture into the home. Thus, young people were being exposed to new values and a peer culture that parents could not control. Conflicts in the 1950s over certain elements of youth culture, such as comic books and Elvis Presley, reflected the fears of parents that they were losing control over their children. Some blamed women's work outside the home for juvenile delinquency, which received a great deal of public attention in the 1950s even though the rates of delinquency did not actually rise during that time (Gilbert 1986).

Despite the image of the 1950s as a placid decade preceding the turbulent 1960s, the youth culture that provoked so much parental concern was a source of rebellion (Breines 1992). Rock and roll music, for example, provided middle-class White teenagers with a connection to Black culture. For New York City teenagers, the beatniks and bohemians of Greenwich Village were a source of fascination (Breines 1992:129). By participating in this culture, teenagers could express their longing for escape from stifling middle-class conventions—even as they also embraced aspects of the dominant culture. Wini Breines writes of her own experience:

> I was both a cheerleader and a beatnik, and while the dissident persona chronologically followed the teen enthusiast during my high school years, they were never clearly separate. Glamor and dissidence, apparently contradictory, both drew me. I still wanted to go to the senior prom and to have all that entailed as I boarded the train for Greenwich Village on Sundays. Popularity mattered even as I donned my black tights. I browsed the

makeup counter in Woolworth's evaluating lipstick and rouge and eyelash curlers. I was hedging my bets, searching for the gaps, exploring the cultural weak spots, trying to sort out what a girl was supposed to be or might be, constructing a feminine identity for the future. (Breines 1992:165)

Although observers of youth culture in the 1950s worried mostly about the rebellion of boys, girls were also expressing discontent about middle-class culture in less visible ways (Breines 1992:129). While rock stars such as Elvis Presley focused attention on masculine rebellion, "girl groups" spoke to teenage girls (Douglas 1994). The Shirelles, for example, were four Black teenage girls who sang the hit song "Will You Still Love Me Tomorrow" in 1960, expressing "the contradictory messages about female sexuality and rebelliousness" that girls were receiving (Douglas 1994:87). Changes in gender relations were occurring, and the changes were both exhilarating and frightening; women and girls were both conforming to traditional expectations and rebelling against them.

Some cultural trends presaged the coming of feminism. For example, movies such as *Breakfast at Tiffany's* featured nonconformist women, and new styles, such as the short hair worn by some actresses, were a form of "gender bending" (Douglas 1994:104). Beatlemania was an outpouring of female sexual energy in which "girls congregated in public in packs, in swarms, waiting for tickets, waiting for concerts, waiting for the Beatles themselves, united in a determined, shared cause" (p. 120). Later in the 1960s, some of these same girls would form a women's liberation movement.

Conclusion

Widespread social changes have helped to transform family and gender relations. They have also raised concerns about social stability and values among men and women. Historically, the family has been an important symbol of stability and traditional values in the face of social change. In the nineteenth century, as industrialization and urbanization disrupted lives, many people sought comfort in the idea that women were creating domestic havens of virtue and support for families. Many women embraced maternalist ideologies, emphasizing their differences from men, even as they extended their roles outward from the home and into the community.

In the twentieth century, social changes have created a mix of lifestyles and values. The entry of large numbers of women into the labor force has been critical in creating new gender expectations. However, women's experiences in the workforce have varied by race and class. Some women have had access only to low-paying service jobs; others have competed with men in careers. Meanwhile, men have found it increasingly difficult to prove themselves in the work world but have also had trouble returning to the family. Thus traditional homemaker and breadwinner roles have come to coexist with new models of family and gender relations.

The major social and economic changes of the nineteenth and twentieth centuries created the potential for a rise in feminist consciousness and for conflicts over gender and family. Cultural phenomena like television both reflected and influenced public sentiments about the changing roles of men and women. However, it was men's and women's participation in social movements that led to the explicit development of feminist consciousness, as we will see in Chapter 3, and to the conflicts over gender and family that we will explore in later chapters.

3

Social Movements and Feminist Consciousness

Major changes in men's and women's lives, such as women's entry into the labor force, do not automatically create gender equality or even widespread awareness of inequality in gender relations. Gender is, after all, deeply embedded in all sorts of social institutions. Even though the majority of American women work outside the home, for example, they still take unequal responsibility for child care. What will it take, then, to change our ideas about what is "natural" for men and women? How do people develop an awareness of gender inequality? What prompts them to start to talk about changing relations that are widely perceived to be "normal"?

In this chapter, we will address these questions by looking at six social movements that promoted the growth of feminist understandings and women's movements. Each movement operated within a particular historical context in which social and political conditions both facilitated and limited change. As these cases show, social movements have been important in generating consciousness about gender relations that has sometimes inspired large numbers of people to work for change. They have also stimulated countermovements and intense battles over issues related to gender and family, as we will see in subsequent chapters.

Varieties of Feminist Consciousness

Broadly speaking, feminist consciousness is the understanding that women have been discriminated against on the basis of their sex and that fundamental social change is needed in order for women's interests and needs to be met. Historically, however, diverse versions of feminist thought have coexisted, even among people who have shared a unifying feminist goal. For example, although campaigns for women's suffrage united women within a number of countries, some women argued for women's suffrage on the grounds of fairness or justice, and others argued on the grounds that women ought to be allowed to spread their highly moral influence through the vote (see Kraditor 1965). Black women in the United States were interested in women's suffrage in part because it would help redress the disenfranchisement of Black men (Cott 1986:52–53). In contemporary times, women who differ by class, race, sexual orientation, and other characteristics continue to hold disparate feminist understandings. Moreover, differences among both women and men based on class, race, and other factors have produced different types of political activity around gender.

One fundamental difference in perspective that runs throughout the history of feminist thought is the debate over women's "sameness" to or "equality" with men versus their "difference" or "special contributions" (see Black 1989; Chafe 1991; Cott 1987; Tong 1989). Feminists who take an "equal rights" perspective believe that women are essentially the same as men and should be treated equally. Those who argue for "difference" maintain that women, by either nature or socialization, are essentially different from men in positive ways that should be promoted; women share such qualities as a capacity for caring and compassion and can make special contributions to society as a result. In this perspective, women also have special needs, owing to both sex discrimination and their distinctive roles, such as mothering. In practice, feminism has always affirmed both "women's human rights and women's unique needs and differences" (Cott 1987:49). Changes in gender relations have come about through a wide range of women's activities (and some men's activities as well), based on a mixture of ideas. Because feminist visions of social change may be more or less attractive to the majority of people at various times, organizations and activities that are inclusive of a wide range of women's experiences may produce more change and engender less opposition than those based on a narrow form of feminist consciousness (see Black 1989).

Women and Temperance Movements

Temperance movements arose in a number of countries in the nineteenth century, including the United States, Canada, Great Britain, Australia, and New Zealand (see Chafetz and Dworkin 1986). In America, alcohol was readily available and was used heavily following the War of Independence (Gusfield 1966). Many temperance societies were organized in

the early nineteenth century with the aim of encouraging either absti-
nence or, at the least, moderate drinking. Later in the nineteenth century,
when "moral suasion was admitted to be an ineffective weapon," the
movement increasingly sought coercive legal solutions, such as local pro-
hibitions on alcohol and a national Prohibition amendment (Bordin
1981:8).

Temperance societies attracted both men and women, but because
"drink was seen to present a threat to the home, both men and women
perceived temperance as a woman's issue" (Bordin 1981:4–5). Particularly in the period after the Civil War, when the Women's Christian Temperance Union (WCTU) was founded, temperance societies became an
important public venue for women's activity. In the United States and
elsewhere, the temperance movement helped to generate feminist consciousness and alter gender roles.

How temperance movements could have undermined traditional
gender relations is something of a puzzle. The American temperance
movement was very closely tied to evangelical religious culture, which is
today associated with right-wing politics. According to Joseph Gusfield
(1966), the crusade against drinking was a reaction to urbanization and
immigration by small-town Americans who found their social status declining. After the failure of Prohibition in the United States, the remaining
members of the dwindling Women's Christian Temperance Union
seemed downright quaint to many Americans. As a local WCTU leader
told Gusfield, "The public thinks of us—let's face it—as a bunch of old
women, as frowzy fanatics. I've been viewed as queer, as an old fogy, for
belonging to the WCTU" (Gusfield 1955:228).

Certainly, the temperance movement did not set out to alter existing
gender arrangements. Rather, women were acting in their roles as mothers
and guardians of social values to try to force men to act responsibly in
their roles as husbands and fathers. The movement was also very much
connected to the religious culture of the time (Giele 1995:64). Temperance
meetings featured prayers, hymns, and references to scripture, and the
organization of the movement was connected to women's participation
in church services, prayer meetings, and missionary work. These connections to existing culture helped the Women's Christian Temperance Union become a large organization with great appeal to many women.

Through an examination of the contents of the WCTU newspaper, sociologist Janet Giele (1995:68–73) shows that the gender ideology of the
temperance movement differed from that of "equal rights" feminists who
were working for women's suffrage in the nineteenth century. Temperance women did not aspire to the roles of men; they saw men as subject

to corruption and temptation, whereas women were strong and morally upright. Their goal was to improve men by extending women's influence from the family to the community. Temperance women had an image of an ideal society that they wanted to achieve, and they were concerned about a wide range of social problems, such as women's working conditions, child labor, education, and the victimization of women who were married to drunkards (Giele 1995:71–72). They believed that they had to exercise social responsibility to combat these problems through charitable activities and temperance work. They did not envision major changes in social institutions or in women's position but focused on uplifting the individual, an approach that was highly compatible with their religious heritage (p. 84).

Despite this conservative gender ideology, the temperance movement made important contributions to changes in gender relations. First of all, the sheer number of women mobilized by the temperance cause is significant. By the 1880s, the WCTU had spread to a number of countries as well as to every area of the United States. The WCTU had attracted nearly 150,000 members in the United States by 1892, compared to the approximately 13,000 members of the National American Woman Suffrage Association (Bordin 1981:3–4). The temperance movement brought large numbers of women out of the home to become involved in the public sphere, and this alone represented an important shift in gender roles (Giele 1995:93). Whereas the American women's rights movement that arose in the nineteenth century was too radical for many women, the temperance movement attracted large numbers because it was compatible with existing values (Bordin 1981; Epstein 1981).

Temperance work also raised women's consciousness in a number of ways. Through their temperance and charitable work, women became aware of a broad range of social issues and pushed for a variety of social reforms, helping to create welfare states in a number of Western countries (Koven and Michel 1990). In Chicago in 1889, for example, the WCTU was sponsoring

> two day nurseries, two Sunday schools, an industrial school, a mission that sheltered four thousand homeless or destitute women in a twelve-month period, a free medical dispensary that treated over sixteen hundred patients a year, a lodging house for men that had to date provided temporary housing for over fifty thousand men, and a low cost restaurant. (Bordin 1981:98)

Before 1873 most women had been active only in their churches, but by 1900, as a result of joining the WCTU, "they had a full generation's experience behind them in political action, legislation, lobbying, and running private charitable institutions" (Bordin 1981:157).

Temperance work made women realize that they were restricted in their ability to bring about change. Temperance activists quickly found that women lacked influence with legislators because they did not have the vote. Consequently, the movement came to endorse women's suffrage and was very important in pushing for this expansion of women's rights:

> It is true that the WCTU couched its feminism in moderate and conciliatory language, in part because of its long involvement with churches and the Prohibition party. But it is also true that the political agenda of the WCTU led forward rather than backward. Its organization and membership in many places kept suffrage sentiment alive when the official suffrage associations were tiny or nonexistent. (Giele 1995:107)

Temperance women did not alter their conception of themselves as mothers and homemakers; they saw the temperance movement as a way of providing "organized mother love." Yet women were gaining a world of new experience through their participation in a social movement. Because of their experiences in the temperance movement, large numbers of women not only supported women's suffrage but also became concerned about issues that still concern feminists today, such as the sexual exploitation of women and violence against women. In the WCTU, they also experienced female collectivity and power (Epstein 1981:131), an experience similar to that felt by contemporary feminists. Even if they did not intend to do so, temperance women expanded their gender roles and their consciousness through social movement activity.

The Abolition Movement and Women's Rights

Another nineteenth-century social movement that helped change gender relations was the abolition movement. Antislavery organizations first became prominent in the United States in the 1830s, after William Lloyd Garrison began publishing his abolitionist paper, *Liberator,* in Boston in 1831 (Kraditor 1969). The American Anti-Slavery Society was founded in late 1833. The movement attracted a diverse group of crusaders, including African Americans such as Frederick Douglass and Sojourner Truth, whose antislavery activities put them at great risk (Leach 1993:2208). Women were present at the founding meeting of the American Anti-Slavery Society, and they formed separate women's clubs within the national society to assist in raising money and circulating petitions.

Two sisters from a slave-holding family in South Carolina, Sarah and Angelina Grimké, began lecturing on abolitionism in 1837, attracting large crowds of men as well as women. Their lectures were so successful that the Grimkés began "traveling from town to town usually in response to invitations from ladies' antislavery societies, something women simply did not do in those days" (Kraditor 1969:42). In response, ministers began criticizing the sisters for their public activities, which were regarded as improper for women, sparking an early debate over women's rights.

Many women who participated in the abolition movement eventually became women's rights activists. They expressed a much more explicit feminism, based on ideas of equality, than did temperance supporters. Some scholars have argued that the abolition movement raised women's consciousness about gender as they compared their position to that of Black slaves (Hersh 1978). Others suggest that many female leaders came to the abolition movement with a preexisting feminist consciousness (see Buechler 1990:19–20). It seems likely that participation in the abolition movement both created feminist consciousness in some women and maintained or expanded it in those who were already thinking about their situations as women because of their experiences in education and voluntary work outside the home.

Women did experience barriers to their public participation within the abolition movement. As the experience of the Grimké sisters demonstrated, the idea that women's place was in the home was so entrenched in nineteenth-century America that it was considered improper for women to speak in public. However, women felt it was their moral duty to speak out against slavery despite the rebukes. At the World Anti-Slavery Convention in London in 1840, women were refused delegate status and forced to sit in the gallery. At this event, two women who would become famous women's rights advocates, Elizabeth Cady Stanton and Lucretia Mott, apparently met and discussed women's rights (Sinclair 1965:57). They decided to organize the world's first women's rights convention, which eventually took place at Seneca Falls, New York, in 1848. The abolition movement certainly increased the networks that existed among women and also enhanced the speaking and organizing skills of female activists.

Drawing on abolitionist rhetoric, women's rights activists developed ideas about justice and equality for women that were missing from the implicit "difference" feminism of the temperance movement. Although the movement was largely White and middle-class, some working-class women and African Americans made important contributions (Leach 1993:2211). At an 1851 women's rights convention, the former slave and abolitionist Sojourner Truth gave a stirring reply to a clergyman who said women were too weak to vote:

> Look at my arm! I have ploughed and planted and gathered in barns, and no man could head me—and ain't I a woman? I could work as much and eat as much as a man—when I could get it—and bear the lash as well! And ain't I a woman? I have born thirteen children, and seen most of 'em sold into slavery, and when I cried out with my mother's grief, none but Jesus heard me—and ain't I a woman? (Quoted in Flexner 1959:91)

Men, too, were involved in the women's rights movement. At the World Anti-Slavery Convention, William Lloyd Garrison sat with the rejected women delegates in the gallery (Sinclair 1965:57). Garrison and numerous other male reformers were firm supporters of women's rights, and many signed the Declaration of Sentiments and Resolutions, the women's rights manifesto modeled on the U.S. Declaration of Independence, at the first women's rights convention in Seneca Falls (Flexner 1959:80). Some women's rights activists, such as Lucy Stone and her husband Henry Blackwell, strived for equality in their own marriages, creating models of new gender relations.

The American women's rights movement that began with the Seneca Falls convention came to advocate profound changes in gender relations. Activists began attacking laws that denied women property rights, custody of children, the right to sue in court, and so forth. They challenged norms such as the prohibition on women's public speech. Although Lucretia Mott's husband was asked to chair the Seneca Falls convention, the women quickly learned to speak for themselves. Elizabeth Cady Stanton, who had experienced the isolation of being a small-town housewife and mother, called for radical changes in family life and women's roles. And women's rights activists came to support suffrage on the grounds of fairness and equality rather than difference.

Because it was challenging fundamental gender roles, rather than building on the dominant culture like the temperance movement, the women's rights movement met with much opposition. For example, activists tried to reform women's dress, introducing a comfortable outfit known as the "Bloomer costume" to replace the tight stays and heavy skirts and petticoats worn by "ladies" in the nineteenth century (see Flexner 1959:83–84). The reform of women's fashion was connected to the effort to expand women's sphere. As Sarah Grimké wrote, "[Men] know that so long as we submit to be dressed like dolls, we never can rise to the stations of duty and usefulness from which they desire to exclude us" (Kraditor 1968:123). Perhaps because the effort to reform women's dress symbolized fundamental change in gender relations, the women received so much ridicule that they were forced to abandon the idea.

Because it was radical, the early women's rights movement attracted a much smaller following than the temperance movement. Nevertheless, the movement helped to produce a larger women's suffrage movement and to change men's and women's consciousness regarding gender. In the end, both the women's suffrage movement, with its emphasis on women's rights as citizens, and the temperance movement, with its emphasis on extending women's role in the home, changed gender relations (Giele 1995).

The Civil Rights Movement and Feminist Consciousness

In the second half of the twentieth century, a wave of new social movements arose in a very different social and political context than that of the movements of the nineteenth and early twentieth centuries discussed above. African Americans had formal legal rights, such as the right to vote, although they were denied these rights in practice in the segregated South. Women were entering the labor force, the universities, and other areas of public life in increasing numbers, although there was still no general support for feminism in the 1950s. It took social movements to change public consciousness about gender relations, and the civil rights movement that emerged in the mid-1950s led the way.

The Student Nonviolent Coordinating Committee (SNCC) was a new civil rights organization that came out of the wave of sit-ins conducted by young southern Blacks in 1960 (see Morris 1984). The Black youths who formed SNCC shared a theology that focused on the goal of a "redemptive community" or "beloved community," in which Blacks and Whites would live together and "demonstrate to the world new possibilities for human relationships" (Evans 1979:37). A handful of mostly southern White women became involved in the civil rights movement and in SNCC primarily through their ties to churches (Evans 1979:35–57). They shared SNCC's moral vision and were excited by the idealism and adventure of the civil rights movement. But as White southern women, they had to struggle with the image of the "southern lady," which they had internalized.

Black women leaders within the civil rights movement were particularly important to these White women as examples of alternative gender roles. Young Black women such as Diane Nash and Ruby Doris Smith courageously led demonstrations, went to jail, and risked their lives for the cause. Outspoken Black "mamas" in the local communities risked their lives to provide food, housing, and support to SNCC activists. Within organizations such as SNCC and the Southern Christian Leadership Conference (SCLC), leaders such as Ella Baker and Septima Clark were dedicating their lives to the movement's vision of justice and beloved community. The examples of all these women "opened new possibilities in vivid contrast to the tradition of the 'southern lady'" (Evans 1979:53). Thus, a small network of women gained a new sense of themselves and of the possibilities for women. They formulated an early feminist perspective that would be influential in circles of activist women elsewhere (p. 57).

The summer of 1964, described by Doug McAdam (1988) in *Freedom Summer*, was a critical turning point for the civil rights movement and was also important to changing gender relations. "Freedom summer" was a project of SNCC, which had been working in Mississippi since 1961 to register Black voters and organize a movement against the blatant racism of the state. The obstacles faced by SNCC in Mississippi were enormous. The governor of the state was a member of the racist White Citizens' Council, as were many judges, police officers, and other government officials. Civil rights workers met with violence on a regular basis, and many local Blacks were too intimidated to press for their rights.

The plan of Freedom Summer was to bring a large number of volunteers, mostly White college students, to Mississippi from the North to register Black voters and to staff "Freedom Schools," which taught subjects such as Black history. One goal of the project was media attention. Another was to get students with influential parents involved as a new source of resources for the movement, and so there was a deliberate attempt to recruit at elite universities such as Harvard and Yale. The project was successful in recruiting about 1,000 volunteers, including some 400 women, despite its enormous risks. Three civil rights workers—James Chaney, Andrew Goodman, and Michael Schwerner—were reported missing just ten days into the project and later found dead, the victims of segregationists led by local police. Although volunteers were aware that they were risking their lives, they were motivated by strong ideals and inspired by the Black civil rights workers who had organized the project.

When the volunteers arrived in Mississippi, some were housed with Black families, who took great risks in sheltering the volunteers. Others lived in the project offices or "Freedom Houses" in communal living arrangements. Volunteers were exposed to the culture of local Blacks and Black SNCC staff. Freedom Summer participants experienced a strong sense of community and commitment to a larger purpose. In the Freedom Houses, the volunteers talked politics, partied, and had sexual relationships, including interracial ones. Influenced by local Blacks and SNCC volunteers, they also adopted new styles of dress and language. Whereas college students in the 1950s and early 1960s wore relatively formal attire on campus, male Freedom Summer volunteers took to wearing blue jeans, a style that had previously been associated with "greasers" or working-class youths. Both male and female volunteers peppered their language with phrases such as "dig it." One volunteer recalled, "I remember my parents freaking out; they thought I had set my education back years!" (McAdam 1982:143).

The cultural innovations of Freedom Summer were important roots of the "counterculture" that developed on many college campuses and elsewhere later in the 1960s (McAdam 1982:138). The volunteers became very much aware of their own struggle for self-liberation at the same time that they struggled for racial equality in the larger society. The project embodied the theme of "the personal as political," which would become central to both the New Left and the women's liberation movement.

Although Freedom Summer was certainly not the only influence on these movements, it was important. When the volunteers returned to the North, they brought with them the cultural experiences and political ideology that they had adopted in Mississippi. Moreover, many of the volunteers returned in clusters to schools such as Harvard, Stanford, Yale, Berkeley, Michigan, Wisconsin, Princeton, and Chicago. There they formed networks of experienced activists. Because of the media attention received by Freedom Summer, "the volunteers returned to school to find themselves regarded as conquering heroes by the small but growing subcultures on their respective campuses" (McAdam 1982:161). Many of the Freedom Summer volunteers became leaders in the student and antiwar movements that were forming on campuses throughout the United States. Many of the women volunteers later became activists in the women's liberation movement. Because of their work in the civil rights movement, these women shared a vision of personal liberation, community, and a more just society that they eventually applied to gender relations.

Some women, particularly Black women, did play major roles in the civil rights movement. Although few were public spokespersons, many were important leaders within organizations such as SNCC. Even White women, such as Mary King and Casey Hayden, had important staff positions in SNCC prior to its Black separatist period in the late sixties. But during Freedom Summer, the female volunteers had experienced various forms of sexism, including both sexual harassment and a double standard with regard to sexuality. In work assignments, the women typically did the clerical work, taught in the Freedom Schools, and staffed the community center, whereas men did higher-status "political work" such as voter registration (McAdam 1982:105–107). At the time, the women did not have the feminist language and ideology with which to recognize and question the sexism in the project, but they were exposed "to the glaring contradiction between the civil rights movement's ideology of equality and the lived experience of inequality" (p. 178). When Doug McAdam interviewed former volunteers 20 years later, they recognized sexism in the project that they had not comprehended at the time.

In the summer of 1964, a small group of Black and White women in SNCC talked about sexual inequality (Evans 1979:84). In November 1964, Mary King and Casey Hayden wrote an anonymous position paper in which they listed some of the incidents that provoked their concern. For example: "Two organizers were working together to form a farmers league. Without asking any questions, the male organizer immediately assigned the clerical work to the female organizer although both had had equal experience in organizing campaigns" (SNCC Position Paper, November 1964; reprinted in King 1987).

In their memo, Hayden and King compared "the assumption of male superiority" in SNCC to the assumption of White superiority in the larger culture. In a second, signed memo written a year later, Hayden and King drew parallels between the treatment of Blacks and women in society. Thus, consciousness about gender inequality was related to consciousness of racial inequality.

In her memoir, Mary King argues that the women were motivated not by complaints about their roles within the movement but by the positive desire to extend the vision of the civil rights movement to gender relations. As she explains:

> we were asking whether we would be able to act out our beliefs and make decisions based on our convictions, beliefs grounded in our definition of freedom and self-determination as women, stemming from what we had learned in the movement. (King 1987:460)

In the civil rights movement, women had learned to act in the public arena to expand human possibilities, a lesson they would next apply to women's liberation.

The New Left and the Rise of the Women's Liberation Movement

Inspired by the southern civil rights movement, a northern student movement developed in the United States in the early sixties. Northern college students organized "sympathy boycotts" and pickets of the chain stores that were targeted by the southern sit-in movement (Miller 1987:34). In addition, northern students formed a new organization, Students for a Democratic Society (SDS), in 1960 (see Sale 1973). Like SNCC, SDS began by stressing the importance of community, personal politics, and "participatory democracy." The organization's manifesto, known as *The Port Huron Statement,* was drafted by Tom Hayden and, after discussion and collective revision, adopted by SDS in 1962. The document stressed the importance of personal freedom and political participation and the need to bring human values to politics (see Miller 1987). Adherents of this approach came to be known as the "New Left."

Despite its emphasis on participatory democracy, the northern student movement was "highly male dominated," and SDS was permeated by the "competitive intellectual mode" of the young men such as Hayden who led the organization (Evans 1979:108–109). Few women were part of the organization's inner circle, which was dominated by informal male leadership groups. Women interviewed years later reported feeling "overwhelmed" and "intimidated" by the male style of the organization, and some were fearful of offering their opinions at meetings (Evans 1979:115).

Nonetheless, women did gain activist experience in SDS and the New Left. They were particularly central to the Economic Research and Action Project (ERAP), in which SDS members moved to the slums of nine American cities to try to organize the poor and pressure governments in the North just as SNCC was doing in the South. Although ERAP faced many obstacles and a number of the local projects soon disbanded, women were central to the most successful projects, such as the Cleveland ERAP. Historian Sara Evans (1979:141) points out that "women provide the backbone of most community-organizing attempts" because they tend to be more directly concerned with concrete issues related to "women's sphere of home and community life," such as schools, housing, and garbage removal. Building on their own interpersonal skills, women organizers in ERAP made connections with local women and became effective organizers within the projects. "While the men futilely tried to organize unemployed men, street youth, and winos, women quietly set about creating stable organizations of welfare mothers"

(Evans 1979:141). As they did so, the women created for themselves "a new sense of potential and self-respect" that was a "basis for female revolt." Out of women's successes in ERAP, "confidence grew in their own ideas," and increasingly, some women "found themselves able to hold their own intellectually as well" (Evans 1979:142).

In December 1965, the memo written by the two SNCC women, Casey Hayden and Mary King, was distributed to participants at an SDS conference, and some women from ERAP led a workshop on the issue of women's role in the movement. The discussion turned out to be the most riveting of the conference: "Small groups—mostly composed only of women but a few including men—engaged in an exciting, searching, angry, and enlightening conversation that continued on into the night and through the next day" (Evans 1979:156). At the conference and in notes circulated afterward, women began to talk not only about their roles within the movement but also about their socialization in the larger society into roles focusing on motherhood and family (p. 165).

At the same time that the "women's issue" was being raised in the New Left, a "counterculture" was blossoming across the country, particularly on college campuses. Students and other young people were examining their own lives and changing their lifestyles, wearing the long hair, beards, jeans, and beads that came to be associated with "hippies" and rejecting the values of materialism and competitiveness in favor of community and cooperation. The counterculture provided one of the bases for women's liberation through its

> rejection of middle-class standards and lifestyles and its focus on personal issues. It called into question basic defining institutions for women such as marriage and the family, asserting in fact that communal living was superior. And it pushed into reality the potential sexual freedom inherent in the pill. (Evans 1979:175)

Although the counterculture brought "new forms of sexual exploitation" (p. 177), which would become targets of feminist anger, it also provided some relief from confining gender roles. Men and women were beginning to discover alternatives to the *Leave It to Beaver*–style family.

Meanwhile, the student antiwar movement began to focus more and more on the military draft, which was used to recruit soldiers for combat in Vietnam. Because women were not subject to the draft (and were not permitted to engage in combat when they joined the military), women found themselves in increasingly peripheral positions in the antiwar movement. Many men had to decide whether to go to Vietnam, burn their draft cards, go to Canada, or go to jail. But in the draft resistance movement, women were expected only to be supportive of men, as suggested by the popular movement slogan, "Girls Say Yes to Guys Who Say No!" (Evans 1979:179). Men stressed the risk-taking, manly character of draft resistance, and "the presence of women, defined as girlfriends, admirers, and bedpartners, was used to buttress an almost swaggering masculine role" (Thorne 1975:184).

Women themselves were torn by feelings that their own concerns were in fact secondary and by resentment of the subservient roles they were expected to play within the movement. Because of their experience of subordination within the draft resistance movement, however, women began to meet in separate groups. They raised the issue of women's status at draft resistance meetings, but were frequently made to feel like outsiders within the movement. As a result, women began to identify themselves with the emerging women's liberation movement (Thorne 1975).

The "woman question" was also discussed at various SDS meetings. However, many women became increasingly alienated from a male-dominated movement that failed to take their concerns seriously. At an SDS meeting in 1967, women presented an analysis of women's oppression that built on New Left rhetoric, comparing women's relationship to men with that of the Third World to its colonizers. They urged SDS to develop programs "to free women from their traditional roles in the family: communal child-care centers, help with birth control and abortion, and equal sharing of housework" (Evans 1979:191). Although the resolution was adopted, there was much conflict over the women's analysis, which some men declared "stupid." In the account of the meeting that appeared in the movement publication *New Left Notes*, the session was reported "alongside a cartoon of a girl—with earrings, polkadot minidress, and matching visible panties—holding a sign: 'We Want Our Rights and We Want Them Now'" (Evans 1979:192). In this and numerous other instances within the antiwar movement, women's concerns were ridiculed (see Freeman 1975).

Women had become aware of their own oppression through their participation in the civil rights movement and the New Left, and they had used the language of these movements to articulate their positions. When they realized that men would not take their concerns seriously within these movements, they decided to form an independent women's liberation movement. Organized by young women who considered themselves "radical" as a result of their prior movement experience, the new women's liberation movement would make militant demands and would question basic assumptions about men's and women's spheres.

Women's Strike for Peace

While young women were discovering the limitations of gender within the civil rights movement and the New Left, somewhat older women, who had embraced the role of housewife and mother, were expanding and questioning their roles as well. Women's peace movements had existed in many countries since the early twentieth century and included international organizations such as the Women's International League for Peace and Freedom (WILPF), which was founded in 1915. During the Cold War, as the threat of nuclear confrontation escalated, new women's peace groups were formed, some of them ignorant of the history of women's peace movements.

Women's Strike for Peace (WSP), which was founded in the United States in 1961, was one such organization. Historian Amy Swerdlow, who was a key activist in WSP, has written a detailed account of Women's Strike for Peace that reveals its importance to changing gender relations. The women who became activists in WSP were mostly housewives who, "like millions of their cohorts in the period after World War II, had given up jobs, careers, professional training, and dreams of personal achievement to become full-time mothers and consenting members of the culture of domesticity" (Swerdlow 1993:233).

WSP was founded by a handful of women who became alarmed when, after a three-year moratorium, the Soviet Union resumed atmospheric testing of nuclear arms and the United States announced that it would do likewise in response. The women decided to call a national peace protest, and on November 1, 1961, thousands of mostly middle-class White women held rallies in Washington, D.C., and in communities across the United States, using the slogan, "End the Arms Race—Not the Human Race" (Swerdlow 1993:1). After this successful debut, WSP was established as a national organization with chapters throughout the country. It attracted large numbers of women, who worked tirelessly and enjoyed some spectacular successes, including a major role in convincing the U.S. government to sign a partial test-ban treaty with the Soviet Union and Great Britain in 1963.

The women who founded WSP and others who joined the organization typically presented themselves as "ordinary housewives" who were acting in the name of motherhood. The founders of WSP were actually a very talented group of women who were politically experienced members of other organizations, such as the Committee for a Sane Nuclear Policy (SANE). They were also affluent, middle-class women who had the leisure time and the means to volunteer for the cause. Most were in fact homemakers and mothers, however, and they used "maternalist" rhetoric to argue for peace, both because it was natural to them and because they believed that such language would be understandable and appealing to the average American woman. Thus, they expressed their outrage as mothers that the futures of their children were endangered by militarism.

The maternal rhetoric of WSP was indeed attractive to ordinary, middle-class women, many of whom became active in the organization. Even Phyllis Schlafly, who later became known for her opposition to feminism, joined WSP in testifying for a test-ban treaty "as a mother who is eager that her five small children have the opportunity to grow up in a free and independent America" (Swerdlow 1993:94). Amy Swerdlow argues, however, that WSP did not set back, but rather advanced, the cause of gender equality. Like the temperance movement, WSP attracted large numbers of women by drawing on the existing culture of domesticity. As women became involved in working for the cause of peace, they experienced their own collective power to influence government and make history. Like members of the Women's Christian Temperance Union before them, many WSP activists also experienced the joy of working in an effective organization of women (Swerdlow 1993:240).

WSP members did not begin their struggle with any background in feminism or any knowledge of feminist theory. When they encountered the second wave of the feminist movement in the late sixties and early seventies, however, they were receptive to its message because their consciousness had been changed by the experience of working in WSP. Through years of political work in an organization of women, WSP participants learned to rely on themselves, rather than on men, and they learned that they could be powerful working together. Swerdlow (1993) notes that

> throughout the 1960s the key women of WSP maintained that they had left their homes only to save the children and that when the political emergencies, such as the nuclear threat and the Vietnam War, were resolved they would return to full-time homemaking. Yet most of the women of WSP never did go home, because when the Vietnam War was over they no longer perceived the home as the center of their lives or responsibilities. (P. 239)

Although the women of WSP had emphasized their roles as mothers in the struggle for peace, they helped

> to change the image of the good mother from passive to militant, from silent to eloquent, from private to public. . . . In a time when the prevailing family ideology confined mothers to family service, WSP stressed the

social, communal, and global obligations of motherhood, thus challenging the feminine mystique under which the WSPers had lived most of their adult lives. (Swerdlow 1993:242)

Because WSP's challenge came at a time when women were leaving the home to join the labor force, it was doubly effective.

The Environmental Movement and Men's Consciousness

Thus far we have seen how an array of social movements helped to generate feminist consciousness in women. Men have also had their consciousness raised through social movement activity. Although some men in the civil rights movement and the New Left ridiculed women's early attempts to raise feminist concerns, many also came to take the ideas seriously, particularly as an independent women's movement gained strength. Since the early 1970s, feminist ideas have influenced both women and men in many different social movements, including anti-nuclear power movements, peace movements, and environmental movements (see Epstein 1991; Meyer and Whittier 1994).

In a study of male participants in the Australian environmental movement, which had a strong feminist presence in the 1980s, Robert W. Connell (1990, 1995) provides an interesting look at how men's ideas about masculinity change as they encounter feminism. Connell conducted "life history" interviews with men in the movement, asking them about concrete experiences in their lives that helped to influence their views of gender. He focuses on the histories of six men who were environmental activists and had been part of the Australian counterculture that emerged in the 1970s.

All of the men in Connell's study had earlier in their lives accepted the dominant model of masculinity, including "such familiar features as competitiveness, career orientation, suppression of emotions, [and] homophobia" (Connell 1990:459). When they became active in the environmental movement, however, the men found that "there was a challenge to conventional masculinity implicit in the movement's ethos and organizational practices" (p. 463). The movement stressed equality among participants in organizational decision-making, solidarity among participants, and an ideology of personal growth, which was part of the larger counterculture in which the movement was situated. When the men encountered feminism within the movement, they came to feel guilty about sexism, which led some to make changes in their own lives. For example, one man who began living with a feminist woman reported:

> Kathy and I did things like swapping roles—she went out to work quite a lot of the time while I stayed home . . . and I'd do all the domestic things, which I really like. . . . I learnt feminism through practice, not through reading about it, which probably makes it a lot more real and a lot more relevant. And for me it was a big change to come in contact with it because it made me realize there was another side to life. The female side to life that I hadn't been experiencing, or taking into account. [Which involves] giving to people, looking after people, those sorts of things. (Connell 1990:465)

Within the environmental movement, men found support for gender role changes that is lacking for men in mainstream Western societies (see Gerson 1993).

Connell points out that the changes exhibited by men in his study were in individual attitudes and roles rather than in institutional structures. Nevertheless, social movements such as the environmental movement do help to spread new ideas about gender relations, and they provide a cultural space for some men and women to practice those ideas. Within the Australian environmental movement and counterculture, men could renounce careers and the breadwinning role; women could gain new experiences beyond the role of nurturant caretaker of men and children.

Other accounts suggest that men frequently encounter feminism within different types of environmental movements and change their outlooks as a result. In the American anti–nuclear power movement of the late 1970s and early 1980s, such groups as the Abalone Alliance, which was formed with the goal of closing down the Diablo Canyon nuclear-power plant in California, were explicitly committed to feminist goals. When the Abalone Alliance created a blockade at the gate of the nuclear-power plant, it set up a camp that became a model of a feminist, egalitarian society (Epstein 1991:111–12).

In the toxic wastes movement, the question of sexism has been raised "because the focus of toxic organizing is home, community, integrity of the family, health—all traditionally women's domains of concerns" (Szasz 1994:152). Women are a majority within the movement, both as members and as leaders, and they have forced men to deal with issues of sexism (see Brown and Ferguson 1995). As a result of the influence of women and other groups, the toxic wastes movement has adopted a broad progressive agenda, which links environmental issues to issues of race, gender, and other matters of social justice.

Change in gender and family relations has also appeared in environmental movements dominated by working-class activists who do not necessarily endorse feminism. For example, in a working-class, community-based environmental movement that was formed in 1980 to stop the pollution of a creek by a tannery, the women expressed support for traditional gender roles with comments such as "We were raised up to believe you're supposed to wait on your husband and your kids" and "You have total respect for the man of the house" (Cable 1992:46). Yet many women gained a new consciousness of their own abilities by participating in the movement. As the women moved away from traditional gender roles, they changed the outlook of their husbands as well. For example, one activist commented:

> I'd carry my husband a cup of coffee and it never bothered me. And then one day [about three years after mobilization] I thought, "He never carries me a cup of coffee. Doesn't he feel about me the way I do about him?" And so I asked him to do things for me to see what his reaction would be. And he was glad to do it. (Cable 1992:46)

Conclusion

In the nineteenth century, urbanization and industrialization helped women to break out of their assigned domestic sphere. In the twentieth century, equally significant transformations of economy and society, such as the creation of new jobs for women and the decline of the birth rate, led to the decline of women's role as homemaker and men's role as breadwinner. Women who were affected by these changes participated in social movements, which helped to create an explicit feminist consciousness regarding gender and family.

One important contribution of movements is a vision of human possibilities that can be extended to gender relations. Although the women who participated in the temperance movement were committed to separate spheres for men and women, they did envision a type of community in which both men and women acted as responsible and moral citizens, and it was in pursuit of this ideal that they expanded their experiences. The abolition movement, the American civil rights movement, and the New Left all envisioned an egalitarian and participatory society, which women took seriously and tried to apply to themselves. Since the 1970s, men have been influenced by the feminist vision that permeates many environmental groups, and they have altered their ideas about masculinity as a result.

Within the mixed-sex movements, women also experienced discrimination, but they did not initially possess the language or theory needed to talk about their grievances and relate them to gender. As they talked among themselves, however, women began to use the rhetoric of these movements to understand their own oppression. At the same time, they drew on their experiences of changing gender relations in the larger society: the networks of educated women looking for outlets for their abilities in the nineteenth century; the entry of women into the labor force and the experience of attending college alongside men in post–World War II society; the mixed messages sent by the mass media; and the new possibilities created by the counterculture of the 1960s. Putting together their experiences in a changing society and the messages of the movements, many women began to develop a feminist consciousness.

Perhaps most importantly, social movement experience gave women a new sense of self-respect and a new confidence in their ability to act in public arenas. In women's organizations such as the Women's Christian Temperance Union and Women's Strike for Peace, women found that they were capable of creating effective organizations without men, and they found the experience of female collectivity highly rewarding. Within mixed-sex movements, women did play important roles, and they sometimes had the experience, as in the ERAP projects, of seeing the value of women's special skills in creating change. In the Australian environmental movement, men learned the value of developing "female" skills and characteristics.

In the rise of feminist consciousness through social movement activity, we see a mixture of ideas about men's and women's "sameness" versus their "difference." The temperance movement and Women's Strike for Peace were effective in appealing to large numbers of women because they built on existing cultural understandings about women's differences from men. Nevertheless, in both cases, the movements expanded feminist consciousness by bringing women out of the home and into a broader community of responsibility. The women who came out of the abolition movement to advocate suffrage and the women who emerged from the civil rights movement and New Left to call for women's liberation had more radical ideas about breaking down men's and women's separate spheres. These ideas alienated many "mainstream" women who felt threatened by them because they were committed to a primary role in the home. Yet the ideas of radical feminists were not all so different from "maternalist" movements such as the women's temperance and peace movements; the very idea of women banding together in a separate movement implies that women have something different to offer (Chafe 1991).

Feminist consciousness, whether of the difference or sameness variety, involves very fundamental gender and family issues. Social movements that promote changes in gender and family relations often provoke strong countermovements. In the following three chapters, we will see that battles over particular issues—the American Equal Rights Amendment, abortion, and gay and lesbian rights—are intense because they symbolize profound changes in gender arrangements related to family life.

4

Feminism, Antifeminism, and the Conflict over Equal Rights

The value of equality has long been embraced by citizens of democratic countries. As an extension of this value, the notion of "equal rights" for men and women also enjoys strong support. Yet support for that abstract value does not always translate into support for feminist initiatives. Women, as well as men, have disagreed as to whether feminism is in their interests. Even when women support many of the goals of the women's movement, they may distance themselves from the label "feminist." In this chapter, we will see how specific feminist goals and the label "feminism" can symbolize broader concerns about gender and family. We will begin with a discussion of the battle in the United States over the Equal Rights Amendment (ERA), which pitted feminists against antifeminists, and conclude with a look at why some young women today reject the feminist label.

The Battle over the Equal Rights Amendment

"Equality of rights under the law shall not be denied or abridged by the United States or by any State on account of sex." That simple statement— together with clauses giving Congress the power to enforce the amendment and specifying that it would take effect two years after ratification— constitutes the entire text of the proposed Equal Rights Amendment to the U.S. Constitution. Suffragist Alice Paul first drafted the ERA in 1920 after the vote for women was won, and the National Women's Party and other women's groups supported the amendment for many years (see Rupp and Taylor 1987). Following the emergence of the contemporary women's movement in the 1960s, the ERA was finally passed by Congress in 1972 and sent to the states for ratification.

On the face of it, the ERA is a seemingly innocuous statement that merely provides a formal affirmation that all women, as well as men, are equal in the eyes of the law; it does not challenge, but rather extends, basic American beliefs in individual rights. Yet the proposed amendment generated a surprisingly fierce conflict between pro- and anti-ERA forces that raged until June 30, 1982, when the deadline for ratification expired and the ERA was defeated.

To understand why the ERA provoked so much conflict, we need to view the ERA battle within the context of the changes in gender and family relations occurring in the second half of the twentieth century. The ERA came to symbolize changes that were applauded by some and feared by others. As increasing numbers of women entered the labor force, men were freed from some of the burdens of breadwinning; as divorce rates soared, women could no longer expect to be supported by husbands throughout most of their lives. For some people, these changes meant freedom from unhappy marriages and restrictive gender roles. For others, the changes created concerns that women and children would be abandoned as men shirked their family responsibilities.

Although majorities of both men and women in America supported the ERA, activists favoring ratification of the amendment were confronted by a determined countermovement opposed to the ERA. To some extent, the conflict between the opposing movements was a battle over family lifestyles and a genuine conflict of interest. On one side were women who were trying to break away from the home and gain political and economic power, together with their male allies. Their goals required widespread change in gender and family roles; if a large proportion of women chose to center their lives around the home, women would never equal men in political and economic power (Mansbridge 1986:100). On the other side were women who wanted to be homemakers and men who agreed that this was women's place. From their perspective, the ERA was not simply a formal legal change but a symbol of objectionable social changes promoted by feminists. If feminists insisted that women must pursue careers, the traditionalists' way of life was indeed threatened. Yet the conflict was also more complicated, involving many aspects of gender and family relations and taking place in a particular historical context.

Support for Equal Rights

When the contemporary American women's movement mobilized in the 1960s, it consisted of two separate branches (see Freeman 1975; Hole and

Levine 1971): an "older" women's rights movement and a "younger" women's liberation movement. One branch was older in that its organizations were formed somewhat earlier than those of the younger branch and because its activists were somewhat older than the women in the other wing of the movement (Freeman 1975). The women's rights branch consisted largely of professional women concerned about employment discrimination. These women organized in the mid-1960s in groups such as the National Organization for Women (NOW), which was founded in 1966. The younger branch, which consisted of many college students and other young women who had been active in civil rights and New Left organizations, formed women's liberation groups in the late 1960s.

From the start, then, the contemporary women's movement was ideologically and organizationally diverse (see Ferree and Hess 1994; Ryan 1992; Whittier 1995). Although the media often portray the U.S. women's movement as White and middle-class, it has in fact received significant support from African-American women and blue-collar women (Ferree and Hess 1994:89). However, different groups within the women's movement have had different priorities. For example, some women of color were offended when NOW tried to organize chapters in minority communities for the purpose of building support for the ERA because they wanted to define their own priorities (Buechler 1990:157).

Although most feminists supported the ERA, the women's movement always included many different voices and no single organization could control the debate. Young women's liberationists typically saw their own priorities as much more "radical" than fighting for the ERA. Older branch women's rights activists became more involved than the younger branch in the campaign for an Equal Rights Amendment. They frequently stressed the values of equality, justice, liberty, and individual rights (Mathews and De Hart 1990:125).

These abstract values were behind much of the public support for the ERA (Mansbridge 1986). In a 1977 survey, for example, 67 percent of people who had heard of the ERA favored it. Yet many of the same people also held traditional views about gender. For example, 66 percent of the sample believed that preschool children would suffer if their mothers worked, and 62 percent believed that married women should not hold jobs when jobs were scarce and their husbands could support them. Just as public tolerance of women's employment in the 1940s did not mean approval of new gender roles (see Chapter 2), public support for the ERA as an abstract right in the 1970s did not imply support for substantive changes in gender roles and the family.

Feminists, however, were interested in substantive changes. Although they were not central to the pro-ERA campaign, the activities and positions of the younger branch of the movement did affect the debate. In the late sixties and early seventies, women's liberationists were questioning basic social institutions such as marriage and arguing for changes such as communal child rearing (see Davis 1991). In public demonstrations, the rhetoric of younger feminists regarding marriage and the family was often strident, and it may have alienated many mainstream American women. For example, in 1969 women's liberationists distributed a pamphlet at a bridal fair that declared, "Marriage is a dehumanizing institution—legal whoredom for women." Later that year, radical young feminists demonstrated outside New York's Marriage License Bureau, using a leaflet that declared marriage an institutionalization of the rape and bondage of women (Mansbridge 1986:102–103; documents in Morgan 1970).

Of course, not all feminists endorsed such views of marriage, and many advocated changes that they hoped would make life better for both men and women (see Friedan 1981). Women's rights activists generally avoided threatening language, but they did challenge existing gender relations in families. For example, NOW's 1966 Statement of Purpose declared: "We believe that a true partnership between the sexes demands a different concept of marriage, an equitable sharing of the responsibilities of home and children and of the economic burdens of their support" (quoted in Mansbridge 1986:99).

NOW's founders "were careful not to take a formal position against the homemaker," and they also included statements of support for homemakers, such as a call for recognition of the social value of housework and child care (Mansbridge 1986:99). Nonetheless, feminists were challenging women's confinement to a place in the home.

Many early women's rights activists were inspired by Betty Friedan's 1963 book, *The Feminine Mystique*. Friedan argued that many American women suffered from "the problem that has no name":

> It was a strange stirring, a sense of dissatisfaction, a yearning that women suffered in the middle of the twentieth century in the United States. Each suburban wife struggled with it alone. As she made the beds, shopped for groceries, matched slipcover material, ate peanut butter sandwiches with her children, chauffeured Cub Scouts and Brownies, lay beside her husband at night—she was afraid to ask even of herself the silent question— "Is this all?" (Friedan 1963:11)

By acknowledging that not all women feel fulfilled by the homemaker role, Friedan provided legitimation for working women and helped housewives who felt unhappy to understand that they were not alone. Particularly around 1970, when the women's movement received a great deal of media attention, many housewives joined groups such as NOW. For both housewives and employed women in the women's movement, the Equal Rights Amendment came to symbolize women's desire to live to their full human potential.

Some women who had previously embraced the "feminine mystique" became open to the ideas of the women's movement. Women's Strike for Peace members first encountered young feminists in 1967, when they participated in a women's antiwar coalition called the Jeannette Rankin Brigade (JRB). The women's liberationists were openly critical of the WSPers for their use of maternal rhetoric. The conflicts with the young feminists that resulted were "provoking, frustrating, and even confusing, but for some WSP women they were also a transformative experience, one that changed our lives" (Swerdlow 1993:137). At a "countercongress" called by the women's liberationists after a protest at the Capitol, young women spoke "about the way in which the traditional women's peace movement condoned and even enforced the gender hierarchy in which men made war and women wept" (p. 140). Although WSPers were dismayed that attention was being diverted from the war, Amy Swerdlow recalled that the event "left many of us with a great deal to think about" and "provoked heated debates about traditional sex roles, the meaning of woman power and women's liberation, and whether or not affluent young radical women had the right to push their demands forward when our sisters were dying in Vietnam" (p. 140). When the leftist magazine *Ramparts* carried a front-page picture of a women's peace protester, showing only her JRB button and half-exposed breasts, and ran a story that failed to seriously discuss the coalition's purpose, the feminist consciousness of many WSPers was raised (pp. 140–41). Although "motherist consciousness" continued to dominate many WSP actions, the group also began to use some feminist rhetoric, and many WSPers became committed feminists.

Thus, the battle over the ERA was never simply one of housewives versus career women. Not only did significant numbers of housewives become feminists, but opinion polls consistently showed that more housewives supported the ERA than opposed it (see Daniels, Darcy, and Westphal 1982). Nor was the battle simply one of men versus women; majorities of men also supported the ERA, and some men were themselves rebelling against the restrictions of traditional gender roles (Ehrenreich 1983). It is true, however, that women in the labor force were more likely to support the ERA than either men or housewives. Moreover, the gap between employed women and homemakers on gender issues widened somewhat during the years of the ERA battle, with housewives taking more traditional positions than employed women (Mansbridge 1986:204, 216–17). Opponents of the ERA portrayed themselves as housewives and made the ERA into a symbol of threats against traditional family life.

Opponents of the ERA

The ERA was passed with strong support in Congress in March 1972. It was quickly ratified by 22 state legislatures in the same year and was expected to easily be ratified by the 38 states needed to put the amendment into the U.S. Constitution. After 1972, however, the ERA was approved by only 13 additional states, and 4 states voted to rescind passage of the amendment (Boles 1979:3). Although the deadline for ratification of the ERA was extended from 1979 to 1982, the amendment ultimately went down to defeat. Despite support for the ERA from many organizations and national figures and support by a majority of the public in opinion polls, the ERA was thwarted by strong opposition.

The anti-ERA movement was able to build on a conservative base of support that included many religious fundamentalists (see Arrington and Kyle 1978; Brady and Tedin 1976; Tedin et al. 1977). Phyllis Schlafly, the founder of Stop-ERA, the major organized force against ratification, had long been active in conservative politics. In 1972 she published her first attack on the ERA in her newsletter, *The Phyllis Schlafly Report*, and used its readers as the base for her national campaign against the ERA (Mathews and De Hart 1990:50). Schlafly quickly joined forces with Senator Sam Ervin, the chief opponent of the ERA in Congress, convincing him to use the resources of his congressional office to send out antiratification materials and act as "a national clearinghouse and communications center for the opposition" (Mathews and De Hart 1990:51). Anti-ERA leaders frequently came from right-wing organizations such as the John Birch Society, the Eagle Forum, and Daughters of the American Revolution (Mathews and De Hart 1990:153). Opponents of the ERA also organized numerous ad hoc groups in the states, such as Women Who Want to Be Women in Texas and Right to Be a Woman in Illinois (Boles 1979:79–80).

The anti-ERA movement attracted a constituency of women who found social changes such as the rising divorce rate extremely upsetting. Anti-ERA activists believed in the "right to be a housewife," and they saw the ERA as releasing men from their responsibility to support their wives and children. In a careful review of laws that were on the books in 1972 when the ERA battle began, Jane Mansbridge (1986) concludes that the ERA would actually have benefited housewives financially in some ways. For example, it would have given them a veto over the disposition of community property in states with community property laws. But affluent women would probably have been subject to the same financial obligations as husbands, and men may have had an easier time challenging the presumptive rights of mothers to custody of children (Mansbridge 1986:96). By 1982, the law had changed substantially in these areas even without the ERA, and Mansbridge concludes that the amendment would have had little impact on homemakers. However, it was not the real but the symbolic effects of the ERA that were important; "what was at stake in the battle over the ERA was the *legitimacy* of women's claim on men's incomes" (Ehrenreich 1983:146). The ERA became a symbol of changing lifestyles and the decline in social status accorded to the housewife role.

Some women opposed to the ERA feared changes that might disrupt existing, comfortable gender roles. For example, one ERA opponent wrote to Senator Ervin about why she wanted to maintain her current relationship with her husband:

> He works for me, takes care of me and our three children, doesn't make me do things that are hard for me (drive in town), loves me and doesn't smoke, drink, gamble, run around or do anything that would upset me. I do what he tells me to do. I like this arrangement, it's the only way I know how to live. (Quoted in Mathews and De Hart 1990:160)

Other women expressed fears that they were too old to change roles or too unprepared to enter the labor market. From their perspective, the ERA would deny women traditional choices rather than expand their freedom.

Opponents of the ERA also feared changes in parent-child relations, which they associated with the amendment. As Chapter 2 explained, youth culture expanded significantly in the postwar era, reducing parents' control over their children's values and behavior. ERA opponents believed the women's movement advocated goals that would create more undesirable changes in parent-child relations. Furthermore, the women's movement came on the heels of other social movements, such as the civil rights movement, that had already forced changes disturbing to some. ERA opponents feared

> government-supported child centers that under ERA would take children away from their families just as busing had literally taken children away from their families in the process of desegregation. Having already seen

family life put at risk by policies identified with racial equality, many women were apprehensive about what a federal commitment to sexual equality would mean. (Mathews and De Hart 1990:156)

ERA opponents saw a threat to parental control in feminists' efforts to purge school textbooks of "sexism" and references to traditional gender roles. And "ERA symbolized commitments by schools and universities to wean sons and daughters away from their parents" (Mathews and De Hart 1990:156).

The social movements of the 1960s were fresh in the minds of anti-ERA activists. Socially conservative women tended to view the 1960s and feminism as symbols of moral decay (Klatch 1987). After all, the youth movement of the sixties had challenged traditional lifestyles, advocating sexual freedom and collective alternatives to the family, for example. The 1960s had also brought an emphasis on "rights," which many social conservatives saw as an abdication of social responsibility in favor of self-interest (Klatch 1987:121). Feminism, in the conservative view, extended this challenge to the family. In the words of Phyllis Schlafly, women's liberation implies "liberation from home, husband, family and children" (quoted in Klatch 1987:130).

In seeking their own self-fulfillment outside the home, feminists were seen by many ERA opponents as devaluing the role of the homemaker. One antifeminist activist complained:

> The women's liberation movement looks down on the housewife. She should be the most respected person as she is bringing up future generations. But women's liberation puts her down and says, "All she does is stay home all day and wash dirty diapers." ERA won't do anything for these women. (Quoted in Klatch 1987:132)

Moreover, the feminist pursuit of new roles for women outside the home was seen as competing with the homemaker role, eliminating women's choices. An anti-ERA leader explained:

> The women who used to say, "I'm a homemaker" with pride now say, "I'm just a housewife." That's a terrible change in attitude. I don't think that's good at all. Why it's really unfortunate is because girls getting out of college don't get the choice. They think they have to make long-range career plans. They have to go to graduate school. . . . They have to keep a job. They put their children in daycare centers. (Quoted in Klatch 1987:131–32)

Because homemaking is so devalued by feminists, social conservatives argued, women can no longer choose traditional gender roles; new lifestyles for women necessarily compete with the old ones (Klatch 1987:133).

Antifeminist concerns also revealed an underlying distrust of men (Ehrenreich 1983; Klatch 1987). In an age of high divorce rates, a woman with limited earning power might well have "a terrifying sense of her own vulnerability" (Ehrenreich 1983:146–47). Phyllis Schlafly warned:

> Consider a wife in her 50's whose husband decides he wants to divorce her and trade her in on a younger model. This situation has become all too common, especially with no-fault divorce in many states. If ERA is ratified, and thereby wipes out the state laws that require a husband to support his wife, the cast-off wife will have to hunt for a job to support herself. . . . The most tragic effect of ERA would thus fall on the woman who has been a good wife and homemaker for decades, and who can now be turned out to pasture with impunity because a new, militant breed of liberationist has come along. (Quoted in Klatch 1987:136)

Men, in this view, must be legally required to do the right thing by women. Antifeminists feared the male shirking of responsibilities promoted by images of masculinity such as those in *Playboy* and blamed the women's movement. According to Mrs. Billy Graham, feminism is "turning into men's lib because we are freeing them from their responsibilities. I think we are being taken for a ride" (quoted in Klatch 1987:137).

ERA opponents and other "pro-family" activists were similar to the temperance activists of the nineteenth century in their attempt to protect women's security and values, but their relationship to the women's movement was completely different:

> Like today's pro-family crusaders, the temperance activists saw themselves protecting "Christian values" and the sanctity of the home, as well, of course, as the security of women. The difference—and it is a decisive one—is that when women organized to protect their status as wives in the nineteenth century they had no trouble making common cause with the feminist movement of their time. . . . [T]he mainstream suffrage movement did not question the division of the sexes into breadwinners and homemakers and took pains to demonstrate that the ballot would not compromise women's ability to cook, sew or comfort her work-weary provider. (Ehrenreich 1983:150–51)

In contrast to the maternalist politics of many nineteenth-century feminists, contemporary women's rights activists sought financial independence for women and, in doing so, threatened financially dependent women (Ehrenreich 1983:151). At a time when the security of the family was threatened by men's rebellion against the breadwinner role, "women chose opposite strategies: either to get out (figuratively speaking) and fight for equality of income and opportunity, or to stay home and attempt to bind men more tightly to them" (pp. 151–52). The ERA became symbolic of these opposing reactions to social changes.

Equal Rights versus the Security of Tradition

In the battle over the ERA, both feminists and antifeminists addressed issues related to gender and family, but their approaches were quite different. Feminists talked of the frustrations of housewives, and antifeminists expressed the fears of housewives that they would no longer be supported by their husbands (Ehrenreich 1983:148–49). Feminists objected to the double burden of family and work that is frequently shouldered by women with jobs and families (see Hochschild 1989), arguing for increased participation by men in child rearing and housework. Antifeminists were distrustful of men and blamed career women for making women's lives harder. As one woman said:

> All I can see is women with careers who then have to come home and clean
> their house, so all day Saturday or Sunday they are doing housework. All I
> see is women taking on men's roles, but not men helping. On one side of
> the feminist's mouth they call for universal daycare, and on the other they
> say, "Don't worry. Men will help." But I don't see men helping. (Quoted in
> Klatch 1987:138)

Both feminists and socially conservative women were concerned about women's interests, but they had very different views of what it means to be female (Klatch 1987:139). Feminists desired freedom from restrictions based on sex, but their opponents saw the division of the world by sex as natural and even sacred (Mathews and De Hart 1990:163). Many anti-ERA activists belonged to fundamentalist Christian churches and based their opposition to the ERA on religious views of gender roles. For example, two anti-ERA activists in Illinois explained their opposition to the amendment in religious terms:

> I believe God made us different. . . . My religion strictly says women should
> submit to their husbands. It says so in the Bible, and you can't believe part
> of the Bible but not all.
>   I know that God gave men certain responsibilities and He gave women
> responsibilities. The men were to take care of the women. . . . "The husband is the head of the wife, as Christ is head of the Church." (Quoted
> in Mansbridge 1986:175)

Beyond such religious justifications, traditional gender relations were viewed as essential to the social order. Just as many people looked to "true women" for stability in the changing world of the nineteenth century, social conservatives saw gender roles as creating order in the face of widespread social and economic changes. By seeking to prohibit discrimination "on account of sex," the ERA threatened to destroy the security of traditional gender roles and to further the dismantling of social rules and boundaries begun in the 1960s (Mathews and De Hart 1990:164). When gender roles were thrown aside, nothing would be sacred.

Anti-ERA activists even suggested that the ERA would lead to the integration of public restrooms. ERA proponents mocked the "potty issue" as absurd, and the argument may have hurt the anti-ERA movement (Mansbridge 1986:114). Yet concerns about integrated toilets echoed anxieties about integrated classrooms in the civil rights struggles of the 1950s and 1960s (Mathews and De Hart 1990:165). Once again, taken-for-granted social boundaries and hierarchies were being challenged. The imagined intrusion on women's toilets was also a symbol of the socioeconomic and sexual vulnerability felt by many women in a rapidly changing world. Just as men could desert their wives and children, they could also rape and sexually exploit women. Beyond these concerns, the toilet issue symbolized what antifeminist women wanted to preserve about being female:

> The ladies' room was a haven and sanctuary. The men's room was a latrine and urinal. To charge that ERA would integrate toilets was to say that women's washrooms would degenerate into men's rooms. The reality of women's sexual distinctiveness, relative weakness, and sense of vulnerability seemed to be starkly highlighted by the unforgiving brutality of a flourescent feminism. The movement had denied the relevance of sexual distinctiveness despite the reminder of that fact in daily acts of purifying and expurgation. (Mathews and De Hart 1990:165–66)

The idea of "unisex" toilets, together with the possibility of other frightening changes such as the drafting of women into the armed services, symbolized to ERA opponents a denial of distinctions on the basis of sex. Yet gender distinctions were at the core of the self-identities of many antifeminists and fundamental to their worldview. For Senator Ervin, who argued against the ERA in Congress, "rational" distinctions between men and women were based on "physiological and functional differences." Men protected women, and women ensured social morality. These differences were no less than the bases for civilization (Mathews and De Hart 1990:36).

Many antifeminist women declared themselves "pleased to be women" and expressed resentment at "women's lib" for trying to deny them this pleasure (Mathews and De Hart 1990:166). One woman who wrote to Sam Ervin told of her great fear of what the world would be like if her "three little girls" could not be raised as girls (pp. 162–63). Feminists were frequently portrayed by anti-ERA activists as "women who want to be men"; by aspiring to masculine jobs and assuming characteristics such as competitiveness, they were rejecting femininity and the more civilized "social sensibility of women." The competence, confidence, and self-assertion that feminists so valued were often interpreted by antifeminists as masculine and a betrayal of the femininity that is the basis for traditional solidarity among women (Mathews and De Hart 1990:167–68).

In short, the battle over the ERA was infused with symbolism. Feminists saw the ERA as a symbol of women's equality and the struggle to realize their human potential, even though the amendment would probably not have produced far-reaching changes (Mansbridge 1986). Antifeminists viewed the ERA as a symbol of all of the threats to their way of life that were besieging them, such as divorce, the increased independence of children, the decline of the breadwinner role, and the movement of women into the labor force. Both camps were reacting to the large-scale social changes of the twentieth century, but their reactions were very different.

Responses to Feminism in the 1980s and 1990s

Around the mid-1980s, the popular press began discussing the "post-feminist" generation of young women, which supposedly rejected the women's movement. According to Susan Faludi (1991), there was also a broader "backlash" against the women's movement, which was blamed for problems such as infertility among women over 30 and a "man shortage." These and other claims about the deleterious effects of feminism are easily disputed, but they do highlight the fears generated by the perceived gains of the women's movement. In particular, some men seem to feel that feminism threatens their masculinity, which they consistently define in surveys as the ability to provide for one's family (Faludi 1991:65). Given the decline in recent years in men's real income and the increased need for women's wages in families, men are less and less able to act as breadwinners. It is not surprising that many blame feminism, with its emphasis on economic equality, for this problem. As we have seen in the battle over the Equal Rights Amendment, some women also interpret feminism as an attack on men's breadwinning role and on their own "right" to be homemakers.

Nevertheless, feminism enjoys solid public support. Surveys reveal that between 25 and 35 percent of American women consider themselves "feminists." Some commentators interpret this percentage as low, but it is not, in fact, much lower than the percentages of women who apply mainstream political party categories to themselves (Mansbridge 1995:27). In a 1989 Yankelovich poll, for example, 31 percent of women called themselves feminists, 33 percent Republicans, and 37 percent Democrats. When asked about specific issues, majorities of Americans express support for such feminist positions as abortion rights and equal pay, and they agree that women are discriminated against. Women who call themselves feminists and those who do not have few differences over issues. For example, the 1989 Yankelovich poll found that 83 percent of feminists and 81 percent of nonfeminists agreed that job discrimination is an important issue for women; 45 percent of feminists and 43 percent of nonfeminists agreed women should be able to get abortions for any reason; and 93 percent of feminists and 94 percent of nonfeminists felt equal pay for equal work was essential for women (Keene 1991). In short, there is no evidence of a general antifeminist trend in public opinion.

Still, significant numbers of people fear or misunderstand feminism. Anti-ERA activists were drawn from the right wing of the political spectrum and they tended to hold fundamentalist religious beliefs, but they cannot be dismissed as a radical fringe movement. It is important to try to understand how and why large numbers of women "received a message feminists did not intend to send" and responded negatively to feminism (Mathews and De Hart 1990:153). Significantly, some of the same concerns expressed by antifeminist opponents of the ERA are voiced by young women in the 1980s and 1990s who are by no means antifeminists.

Studies of college students suggest that most young women take changes in gender and family relations for granted. Having grown up with working parents, divorce, increased educational opportunities for women, and other changes, they see them as normal (Buschman and Lenart 1996). Many college students, both male and female, expect to combine marriage, children, and careers, although both young men and women expect that wives will make more sacrifices for their families (for example, staying home with sick children) than will husbands (Machung 1989). Female college students often express support for nontraditional gender roles and feminist positions, but they also distance themselves from the label "feminist" (Renzetti 1987). How do we explain why some young women feel this way about feminism?

Meanings of Feminism

Beth Schneider (1987) asked her students to interview either their mother, their sister, or a close friend or roommate about what feminism means to them and about why they would or would not call themselves feminists. Of the 65 interviews taken between 1982 and 1984, the majority (61 percent) were done with college students. Admittedly, the sample is in no way representative of women in general, but the interviews reveal some important patterns. First of all, the young women were not antifeminists; Schneider (1987) reports that the interviews

> reveal substantial agreement with women's movement issues, considerable gratefulness on the part of many of the young women for the older generation's work that allows them to take things for granted, and specific positive recognition of some women's movement institutions and products such as rape crisis centers and the publication *Our Bodies, Ourselves.* (P. 8)

Yet most did not call themselves feminists, and they held some negative associations with feminism.

One prominent theme was that the young women, like anti-ERA activists, perceived feminists to be unfeminine and hostile, particularly toward men. For example, a 21-year-old woman described feminists as

> unfeminine, angry, hostile. Women who are fighting against all aspects of life that are considered female. If women wore bras they took them off. If women wore long hair, feminists cut their hair short. They are angry at anything that has ever been done to them by men. (Schneider 1987:8)

Another woman said:

> Feminists don't like men or other women who like to be feminine. They don't accent their femininity at all. In fact, they cover it up. They seem to be afraid of being women. I think they don't like being female. (Schneider 1987:9)

The young women commonly spoke of feminists as rejecting or hating men and some associated feminism with lesbianism. For example, one woman said:

> Feminists are that part of the female population which has chosen to separate their lives entirely from the lives of men. I don't identify with lesbians or understand them or other women who choose to relate solely to women. (Schneider 1987:13)

A few older women in the sample expressed concerns about the threat to the family posed by feminism; like anti-ERA activists, they feared that feminism would eliminate the choice to be a homemaker. Younger women, as in other studies of college students, did not express such concerns but seemed to take for granted that they would combine careers and motherhood. Instead, they expressed the "fear that being identified with feminists will somehow pose insurmountable obstacles to involvements with men." Schneider argues (1987:19) that the young women seemed to have internalized a "middle-class conception of womanhood." The women typically do not stop to think about what womanhood or "femininity" means, but they take it for granted as a part of their identity. Like the anti-ERA activists who accuse feminists of wanting to be men, the interviewees feel that feminism threatens this core part of their identity that has to do with how they dress, act, and relate to men.

A more recent study of young women's attitudes toward feminism by Melinda Goldner and Kim Dill (1995), based on in-depth interviews with college students and young feminist activists, identifies a continuum of responses to the women's movement. Goldner and Dill try to explain not only why some young women distance themselves from feminism but also why some embrace the movement. In their interviews, they found that most college women expressed feminist views such as support for reproductive rights and equality in the workplace. But few (besides the feminist activists interviewed) identified themselves as feminists without qualification (Goldner and Dill 1995:4–5). However, Goldner and Dill note the difference between disclaiming feminism and qualifying one's support for it. Many of the college women that they interviewed "did not fully reject *or* accept association with feminism" but wanted to explain what feminism meant to them.

As Schneider found through her students' interviews, to some young women feminism implies a rejection of femininity and is associated with deviance from heterosexual norms of womanhood. They associate some positive qualities with feminism, but these seem opposed to the pleasures of femininity. For example, one woman called the side of her "that wants to get ahead" feminist but said that she also had an "old-fashioned" side "that still wants to be a woman and feel feminine" (Goldner and Dill 1995:12). In this view, femininity seems to involve dressing fashionably and relating to men sexually, and feminism seems to deny these prerogatives of womanhood.

Feminist Groups

If feminism has so many negative associations, why, then, do some young women take the risk of becoming active feminists? Young women who become active participants in the women's movement are well aware of the negative images associated with feminism. As one activist put it, feminists are often seen as "just a bunch of dykes wearing flannel shirts . . . burning their bras and hating men" (Goldner and Dill 1995:15).

The reason that young feminist activists are willing to risk such labels is that, by becoming active in movement organizations, they can interact with other women with similar beliefs. They become part of a community of women that provides positive support for feminist ideals and a defense against any negative evaluations from the larger society. Thus, the women's movement nourishes alternative views about gender by creating a community in which feminist beliefs are supported. Through participation in this social movement, young women feel free to proclaim feminist ideas and take on a feminist identity. As one activist noted, "knowing that we're all in it together kind of helps. I don't think I could do it if I were isolated and on my own" (Goldner and Dill 1995:17).

The creation of supportive feminist communities has long been one of the greatest attractions of the women's movement. Within feminist groups, women have expressed their concerns, developed their ideas, and strengthened their commitment to changes in gender relations. Consciousness-raising groups, in which women explored their common experiences as women, were an important means of feminist mobilization in the late 1960s and early 1970s. Women who participated in consciousness-raising groups discussed all kinds of issues related to their daily lives, such as relations with men and with other women, sexuality, standards of female beauty, motherhood, and so on (see Cassell 1977; Shreve 1989). The women's movement was addressing issues close to women's lives, making the idea that "the personal is political" very meaningful. Women also found community in many groups formed around such issues as rape and abortion rights.

Young women today who find their way into feminist groups have similar experiences of solidarity with other women and feminist consciousness raising (Goldner and Dill 1995). In creating supportive communities with shared beliefs, however, the women's movement risks alienating potential constituents who stand outside movement networks. For the majority of young women who do not become active participants in feminist groups, "feminism" may seem unrelated to their personal experiences, even though they support feminist goals. For example, a young woman quoted by Schneider (1987) saw feminists as "angry about issues that seem irrelevant" (p. 9). A woman in Goldner and Dill's sample who qualified her support for feminism said that "radical feminists . . . think that the whole cause of the oppression of women is bearing children. . . . [They want] to have a woman-led society free from male bias. . . . That doesn't pertain to me" (1995:12).

Conclusion

The women's movement has clearly attracted a great deal of support, particularly for abstract ideas such as "equal rights." But even such highly popular goals can generate opposition. Feminism has unintentionally raised fears about gender relations among many potential supporters, including the young women who are essential to the movement's survival. In fact, feminists, antifeminists, and qualified feminists alike are struggling with the uncertainties produced by widespread social changes.

One area of uncertainty has to do with men's and women's roles in the family. For men and women who opposed the ERA, the "natural" roles of breadwinner and homemaker were at stake. Women who were committed to the housewife role felt particularly vulnerable in the face of rising divorce rates and expectations that women would work outside the home. Young women today are more likely to take work outside the home for granted, but they may still sense that women will make more sacrifices than men (see Machung 1989). And for feminists, the double burden of work and family, which tends to fall on women, is also of great concern.

Another area of uncertainty has to do with the meaning of "womanhood" and "manhood." Antifeminist men and women, such as ERA opponents, link "masculinity" to breadwinning and "femininity" to the creation of a secure, noncompetitive sphere apart from the less civilized male world. In this view, men—and feminists—are competitive and confrontational, whereas true women use their interpersonal skills to create a peaceful and caring basis for society. They sacrifice personal ambition for the good of the family and, ultimately, society. The feminine woman is a helpmate to her husband and a nurturant mother to her children. She does not compete with men in the workplace, express anger in public, or act aggressively in pursuit of her own interests.

Ironically, many feminists have also focused on women's differences from men, seeing women as more caring and nurturant. They do not, however, want to limit women's influence to that of helpmate. Rather, they would like to see fundamental transformations in the public world as a result of women's influence. In this regard, "difference" feminists are somewhat similar to temperance activists, except that feminists typically view structural change in institutions rather than individual change alone as necessary. However, the ERA battle was fought on the grounds of "sameness" rather than "difference."

Like antifeminist activists, young women who distance themselves from feminism also see feminists as rejecting "femininity." Young women may admire qualities such as assertiveness and strength, but they also see these qualities as antithetical to good relations with men. For young women who qualify their feminism, the concern with femininity is related to their desire to relate to men sexually and socially, rather than as helpmates in the home. They do not want the baggage of "feminism"— with its (media-generated) associations of lesbianism, man-hating, and ugliness—to interfere with their opportunities for relationships with men. Nevertheless, young women who qualify their feminism do support many feminist goals, including equal rights and reproductive freedom.

The issue of abortion has been particularly important in making feminists out of many young women. At the same time, abortion has created intense battles among groups of men and women, as we will see in Chapter 5. Like the ERA, abortion symbolizes broader concerns about gender and family for many people.

5

Abortion and Family Politics

Since the late 1960s, many countries around the world have reformed their laws to allow women greater access to abortion (see Francome 1984). Yet, in a number of countries, including the United States, debate over abortion rages on. Like the struggle over the Equal Rights Amendment, the abortion battle has been waged by two opposing social movements: an abortion rights or "pro-choice" movement that favors legal abortion and an anti-abortion or "pro-life" movement that equates abortion with murder.

Many analysts have argued that abortion, like the ERA, is a symbolic issue; for both opponents and proponents of legal abortion, the issue represents a larger set of issues related to gender and family. In this chapter, we will examine this argument, considering what abortion means to activists on both sides of the issue in the context of the social changes outlined in Chapter 2. We will see that the two opposing movements are indeed concerned about gender and family issues. But the conflict is more complicated than a battle between housewives and career women.

The Symbolism of Abortion

In trying to explain why the abortion conflict is so intense and enduring, observers have pointed to the clash of values and lifestyles underlying the conflict. Political scientist Andrew Hacker (1979) sees abortion as a battle over sexual behavior:

 People who oppose abortion see themselves as citizens who have paid their dues. They have not only accepted parenthood, but have kept their lusts in check. And they know—even envy—what they have missed. The evidence is all around them, not least on prime-time television. . . . Below them they see the poor, engaging in carefree sex and then getting free abortions. Above them stands a modish middle class, enjoying an array of partners and then putting abortions on credit cards. How can one keep one's children moral with so many examples to the contrary? (P. 22)

In this argument, Hacker suggests that abortion foes are motivated by resentment of others who break the rules and get away with it. He also suggests that parents are upset that they can't control their children's lifestyles, particularly their sexual behavior, and that legal abortion symbolizes this loss of control.

Kristin Luker (1984) also views the battle over abortion as a type of lifestyle conflict. In her study of pro-choice and pro-life activists in California, *Abortion and the Politics of Motherhood,* she interprets the abortion struggle as a conflict between two groups of women over the meaning of motherhood. Women who oppose abortion have committed themselves to the traditional female role of wife and mother. Women who support abortion rights do not reject motherhood, but they see this role as only one part of their lives. In Luker's sample, pro-choice women are highly educated, well-paid career women who are not very religious and have one or two well-planned children. In comparison, pro-life women are less educated, less well-off women who tend to be housewives, are very religious, and have larger families. Luker argues that because pro-life women lack such resources as higher education, they cannot compete in the labor market. Thus they are dependent on their husbands and have a stake in maintaining the housewife role. Pro-choice women, on the other hand, do have resources such as education and higher incomes. They have an interest in legal abortion because it allows them to control their reproduction, which allows them to pursue careers.

How convincing are such arguments about the differences between supporters and opponents of abortion and the symbolic meaning of abortion? In the following sections, we'll examine the historical and social context of abortion disputes in North America to see if arguments about abortion are linked to concerns about larger social changes related to family and gender. We'll also examine some of the survey data to see how attitudes toward abortion correlate with other views and characteristics among both the general public and individual members of abortion rights and anti-abortion organizations.

The Historical and Social Context

Under British common law, abortion was legal if done before "quickening" (the point in the pregnancy when the mother can feel fetal movement). But by the end of the nineteenth century, abortion had been made illegal in every American state, in large part because of a physicians' crusade against the practice. Before the professionalization of medicine, abortions were mostly performed by midwives and "irregular" doctors.

The campaign to outlaw abortion was part of an effort by "regular" doctors, who typically had formal training at the better medical schools and were dedicated to scientific research, to drive irregular doctors out of medicine (Mohr 1978).

Carroll Smith-Rosenberg (1985) argues that the anti-abortion efforts of male doctors and others were an attempt to control "strong-minded" and "self-indulgent" women in a period of social change. Although the nineteenth-century "cult of true womanhood" assigned middle-class women a narrow domestic role, the life of the "bourgeois matron" was actually expanding far beyond the home as a result of education and participation in religious activities and social service (Smith-Rosenberg 1985:224–25). Some responded to such changes by accusing middle-class women of having abortions to shirk family responsibilities and participate in nondomestic activites for their own pleasure (p. 236). For example, one doctor claimed that women sought abortions "simply and solely to give a larger license to selfishness and personal indulgence" (p. 237). Some physicians pointed to social movements of the time, including the women's rights movement, health-reform movements, and the free-love movement, as encouraging abortion. Some expressed racist and xenophobic concerns that White middle-class women were selfishly aborting while immigrants were populating the country.

> In this way the male bourgeois elite—physicians and legislators, editors and their new urban audience—projected the problematic aspects of the bourgeois revolution (the declining birth rate and the sexual restraints birth control necessitated; the breakdown of old customs; the frightening ways of the new cities; the influx of new immigrants; conflict within the medical world; the bourgeois matron's increasingly public persona; the pervasive sense of change out of control) onto the mythologized figure of the aborting matron. They then counterposed her to another of their mythic sexual construction—the True Woman who accepted her biological destiny and gloried in her reproductive sexuality. The aborting matron served as the scapegoat for all that was problematic in the new social order. The dependent and domestic True Woman asserted that, despite its emerging problems, the bourgeois order, rooted in women's biology, was natural and God-ordained. (Smith-Rosenberg 1985:238–39)

Interestingly, a simultaneous female anti-abortion discourse was also reflecting concern about social changes, but it was very different from the male discourse. In sexual and marital advice books written by women between 1870 and 1900, "images of marital rape, of unwanted pregnancies, of marriage as legalized prostitution replaced male images of unnatural aborting mothers and willful urbane ladies" (Smith-Rosenberg

1985:243). These women placed the blame for abortion on husbands who forced unwanted pregnancies on their wives, and they advocated female control over marital sexuality as a means of reducing the incidence of abortion. The concern with male sexual power within the home symbolized a broader concern about male economic and political power and "the constraints and discontents of domesticity" (Smith-Rosenberg 1985:244).

Similar expressions of anxiety over social change emerge in today's conflict over abortion:

> For men, the negative figure of the selfish hard-driving career woman of the late twentieth century expresses, among other things, fears of competition and displacement in the workplace and a retreat from traditional patterns of female nurturance and subservience in the home. (It is perhaps not too farfetched to see the Total Woman, immortalized by Marabel Morgan, as the contemporary equivalent of the nineteenth-century True Woman, who offered men a comforting contrast to the figure of the selfish aborting matron.) For noncareer women, whether in the paid labor force or not, the mythic career woman arouses terrors of economic and emotional abandonment since the former perceive the rules of the game changing in terribly unfair ways. The high visibility of the career woman throughout our culture, able to command a "man's salary," has allegedly weakened the hitherto automatic male willingness to contribute wages to a household once his emotional bond to the woman and children in that household has weakened. (Joffe 1986–87:210)

Although there is no contemporary public discourse equivalent to the nineteenth-century female protest of the "lustful uncontrollable husband," contemporary anti-abortion women do express concerns about male sexual irresponsibility. "Abortion has, in the eyes of these women, made obsolete a social code in which the only honorable outcome of an unwanted pregnancy was marriage or, in the case of the already married, the continuation of a relationship and financial support" (Joffe 1986–87:210–11). Women who want to ban abortion today also want to give women greater control over marital sexual relations. In fact, dissatisfaction with contemporary sexual relations expressed by female anti-abortionists is shared in some ways by feminists who are disillusioned with the "sexual revolution" (Joffe 1986–87:210–11).

In short, changes occurring in gender relations have long been associated with the issue of abortion. In nineteenth-century America, abortion was connected in the minds of many men with the departures of women from "true womanhood," a myth that had provided comfort in the face of large-scale changes such as urbanization and industrialization. In con-

temporary times, abortion is associated with women's work outside the
home, sex outside of marriage, and other lifestyle choices at odds with
"traditional" family life. A strong argument can therefore be made for the
symbolic importance of abortion. Nevertheless, men and women cannot
be easily sorted into two opposing camps: those who stand to benefit
from social change and those who resist it.

Lifestyles, Values, and Abortion

A number of analysts connect the abortion conflict to twentieth-century
shifts in lifestyles (see Markson 1982). Since the 1960s, the availability of
contraceptives and abortion has made it easier to have sex outside of
marriage, and more people are living together without marrying—and
without stigma. Same-sex relationships have also become much more acceptable and visible since the 1960s, challenging heterosexual norms.
And women's roles have changed as women have entered the workforce
and pursued their own interests rather than automatically subordinating
their interests to families. For women, it is no longer prestigious to be a
housewife or to refrain from sex before marriage. Many of these changes
were advocated by social movements that emerged in the sixties, including, especially, the women's movement.

Today abortion not only symbolizes a whole cluster of threatening
values but also is directly implicated in conflicts within families.

> Women's sexuality, the authority of the father, his control of his wife and
> children, parental control over children and the sexual activity of minors
> are all related to this matter [of abortion] in some fashion, and all of these
> relationships are undergoing monumental change at the present time.
> (Rubin 1986:56–57)

Husbands and wives may disagree over whether a pregnancy should be
aborted, and parents may feel that the availability of contraceptives and
abortion limits their ability to control teenagers' sexual activity. For "cultural fundamentalists," abortion thus provides a focus for a set of concerns,
including "sex education, women's rights, teenage promiscuity and
pregnancy, divorce, changing sex and family roles, the secularization of
society, pornography, and the loss of religious values" (Rubin 1986:76).

However, people are not divided on these issues in any simple way.
Men's and women's roles are clearly changing, but the changes are un-
even, creating a diversity of family lifestyles (Gerson 1986–87). In a study
that included women of different social classes, Kathleen Gerson (1985)
found that divisions between "domestic" and "nondomestic" women

were not based on social class or on childhood socialization. Rather, women made choices based on opportunities for work advancement, such as affirmative action programs, and on the circumstances of their private lives, such as the stability of their relationships with husbands or partners. In another study, Gerson (1993) also found men making a variety of choices about work and family commitments in an age when there is no longer a single path to "manhood." When men and women choose more traditional family arrangements, they have different interests than those who adopt newer gender roles and are likely to hold different positions on abortion and a variety of other issues (Gerson 1986–87).

Surveys of the U.S. public demonstrate that most Americans take a middle-of-the-road position on abortion; "they support legal abortions in some but not all circumstances" (Cook, Jelen, and Wilcox 1992:37). Since legalization of abortion in 1973, there has been little change in public attitudes toward abortion. More Americans favor unlimited access to abortion than favor an outright ban on abortion. A narrow majority of the public favors some limitations on abortion. Abortions for "soft" social and economic reasons, such as poverty or the desire of a married couple not to have any more children, have far less support than abortions for "hard" reasons, such as rape or fetal deformity.

Surveys also show that opposition to abortion is associated with other conservative positions on personal morality. Analyses of surveys conducted by the National Opinion Research Center (NORC) show that persons opposed to abortion also want to make divorce more difficult to obtain, do not want to make information about contraceptives available to teenagers, and oppose sex education in schools, pornography, premarital and extramarital sex, and homosexuality. Opponents of abortion also prefer large families and are more religious than supporters of legal abortion. Supporters of legal abortion are likely to have more education and somewhat higher incomes than opponents (Granberg 1978; Granberg and Granberg 1980).

When it comes to attitudes toward women's rights, those who favor legal abortion are more likely to be supportive. When the NORC asked survey respondents if women should stay at home and leave the running of the country to men, if a married woman should work when her husband can support her, if they would vote for a woman for president, and if they thought men were emotionally better suited to politics than women were, supporters of legal abortion were more likely than opponents to take the women's rights position on all the questions. However, comparisons between homemakers and employed women revealed only weak differences in attitudes toward abortion; in every education category, women who work outside the home were only slightly more likely than homemakers to approve of abortion (Granberg and Granberg 1980:259).

In 1980, Donald Granberg surveyed members of the National Abortion Rights Action League (NARAL), a U.S. pro-choice group, and members of the National Right to Life Committee (NRLC), an anti-abortion group in the United States. Among these more active participants in the abortion conflict he found some patterns similar to those revealed by surveys of the general public. Members of the NRLC were much more likely than NARAL members to come from, prefer, and have large families. They were also more likely to be religious, attending church at least once a week, and they were likely to have conservative views on matters of personal morality (Granberg 1981:157).

On the Equal Rights Amendment, there were strong differences between the two groups. Most NARAL members supported the ERA; most NRLC members believed the ERA to be connected to abortion and opposed it. Not surprisingly, on other measures of women's rights, NARAL members were more likely to be supportive than were NRLC members. As Granberg (1981) explains, however, these findings do not mean that the abortion battle is a conflict between feminists and antifeminists:

> In fact, a large majority of NRLC members believe that women should have an equal role with men in running the government and industry and that it is all right for a married woman to be employed outside the home, even if her husband can support her. It is just that the majority taking the more liberal position on women's roles is not as large in the NRLC as in the NARAL. Hence, the intergroup differences are significant. But of the items pertaining to sex roles, only on the issue of the ERA can the two groups be said to be sharply polarized. So, while it is true that NRLC members are more likely to take a traditional view with regard to sex, divorce and birth control than NARAL members, it is not the case that NRLC members are adamantly opposed to everything for which the women's rights movement stands. (P. 161)

The abortion conflict does pit women against women, as the memberships of both NARAL (78 percent) and the NRLC (63 percent) are disproportionately female (Granberg and Denney 1982:41). And there are significant differences between the women; of the married women under age 65 in Granberg's samples, 72 percent of NARAL members are employed full-time, compared to only 19 percent of the NRLC members. Members of both groups have more education and higher incomes than the average American adult (Granberg and Denney 1982:41). However,

NARAL members have only slightly higher educations and incomes than NRLC members, a finding that calls into question the argument that there are important status differences between pro-choice and pro-life activists.

Relying on Granberg's findings and studies of public opinion, historian Keith Cassidy (1995:132) argues that "there is little to confirm the thesis that the root of the abortion conflict is a cultural clash over gender roles—although that may be a factor for some." Cassidy cites analyses of public opinion surveys that find abortion attitudes are not strongly correlated with attitudes toward feminism and gender roles, but are strongly connected to attitudes regarding euthanasia (Cook et al. 1992). Cassidy concludes that "anti-abortion sentiment for many is part of a larger pro-life ideology" (1995:132). He notes that the NRLC does not take positions on issues such as pornography and homosexuality—although some anti-abortion organizations do take positions on such issues—but has focused on abortion, euthanasia, and infanticide out of concern for the absolute value of human life. In contrast, Donald Granberg (1978) has argued against the idea that anti-abortionists hold a more generalized pro-life view because abortion opponents do not also oppose capital punishment and militarism.

In sum, the NORC surveys of the general public and Granberg's surveys of abortion activists provide support for the idea that the abortion issue is part of a larger conflict over lifestyles and values. Supporters and opponents of abortion differ from one another in their views on questions of personal morality. Anti-abortionists tend to be more conservative with regard to sexuality, and they support "traditional" families by opposing easy divorce, for example. Nevertheless, there is no clear split between homemakers and employed women on abortion and other issues. There are also no large socioeconomic class differences between opponents and supporters of legal abortion. Opponents of abortion are clearly more religious than abortion rights supporters, but they are not clearly opposed to women's rights.

The Opposing Movements

The movements on both sides of the abortion issue consist of diverse constituencies. The anti-abortion movement includes many liberal Catholics, who do not take conservative positions on other issues, and it also includes many participants for whom the abortion issue is connected to gender and family issues. The abortion rights movement includes many feminists, but it also includes persons whose primary concern is population control and libertarians who are opposed to government interference in private lives. Even among feminists in the pro-choice movement, there are differences in perspective: Some favor an "individual choice" approach to abortion, and others are more concerned with the larger socioeconomic conditions that affect the decision to have a child (see Staggenborg 1991). Thus, the abortion debate is more than a battle between feminists and antifeminists, employed women and housewives.

Despite diversity in the two opposing movements, not all perspectives receive equal weight in the heat of the abortion battle. At different points in time, particular viewpoints dominate each side. The way in which each side frames the issue depends in part on which constituents are best organized within the movement at the time. Liberal Catholics dominated the early anti-abortion movement in the United States, but fundamentalist Protestants became prominent in the movement in the late 1970s. As a result, the abortion issue became linked to a broader conservative agenda. The framing of the issue also depends on the need to respond to the opposing movement and to attract public support and media attention. Abortion rights supporters have found that an "individual rights" approach to abortion, in which abortion is a matter of personal choice, has broad public appeal as an effective counter to the "right to life" frame. In the following sections we will look closely at the various concerns of participants on either side of the issue and at how the issue has been framed over time.

Anti-Abortion Concerns

An analysis of the Canadian anti-abortion movement by sociologist Michael Cuneo (1989) is particularly valuable in showing the diversity of the movement and the evolution of its ideological perspective. Cuneo, who studied the movement in Toronto between 1969 and 1985, identifies three ideological strands: *civil rights, family heritage,* and *revivalist Catholic* perspectives. He shows how the dominant perspective in the movement shifted over time from a civil rights emphasis to a perspective that combined family heritage and revivalist Catholic concerns. Similarly, the U.S. pro-life movement is complex, but it is currently dominated by the New Christian Right, which has become a potent political force.

Civil Rights Activists

The Canadian anti-abortion movement formed in response to liberalization of the Canadian abortion law in 1969. In the early 1970s, civil rights activists provided much of the leadership of the movement. These activists argue against abortion on the grounds of the humanity of the fetus and the sanctity of human life. They wanted to include opposition to abortion within a larger pro-life framework and to link the movement to other liberal causes such as world peace, economic justice, and racial equality (Cuneo 1989:88).

Civil rights activists are not antifeminists and in fact argue that social structures that discriminate against women and children need to be changed so that abortion will be unnecessary; they would like to make alliances with feminists to achieve these goals. For example, one civil rights activist urged others in the Canadian pro-life movement, "Show the feminists that abortion is a male cop-out in this male-dominated world and that *abortion is not a right for women but, like wife abuse and rape, is a wrong against women*" (Cuneo 1989:95).

This segment of the anti-abortion movement clearly fits Cassidy's characterization of the pro-life movement as concerned primarily with the sanctity of human life. Unlike Luker's sample, however, many of these activists have nontraditional family lifestyles and embrace careers for women.

Although most civil rights activists were Catholics, they deliberately avoided presenting the issue in religious terms so as to appeal to a broader audience. Civil rights activists argued against abortion on the grounds of scientific evidence and the human status of the fetus, "and religious motives of activists were kept under tight wraps" (Cuneo 1989:42). As the movement expanded in the 1970s, however, this strategy began to change because family heritage activists and revivalist Catholics came to outnumber civil rights activists at the grassroots level.

Family Heritage Activists and Revivalist Catholics

Family heritage activists oppose abortion not only because it destroys human life but also because, in their view, it destroys the family and traditional religious values. These activists are outraged by what they see as a pervasive attack on their values, and for them the pro-life movement is a "moral crusade" (Cuneo 1989:85).

Family heritage activists regard abortion as both a symbol and one of the causes of a lifestyle that treats motherhood as something voluntary rather than as the basis of the traditional family and Western civilization. As one family heritage activist remarked:

> Feminists preach reproductive freedom and abortion rights, but what they really want is to deny the majority of women the dignified choice of experiencing the joy of raising kids. This is the most important contribution anyone can make to society, especially today when the consensus is kids stand in the way of material happiness. Feminists just promote the anti-child bias of the times, but where would they or anyone be without women who sacrifice to bring kids up in loving homes? We're the future. The world's very confused, and the only place where genuine values are taught is in the home. (Cuneo 1989:97)

Like the American anti-ERA activists described in Chapter 4, family heritage activists in the Canadian anti-abortion movement viewed the feminist movement as limiting rather than expanding choices for women. It is these activists, Cuneo reports, who best match the profile of anti-abortionists provided by Luker; they are mostly married women who have chosen to stay at home to raise their children.

Revivalist Catholics shared this concern about the traditional family, but they were also upset about what they see as a trend toward liberalism in the Canadian Catholic Church. For these activists, the pro-life cause became a "sacred crusade." Whereas they felt alienated within the mainstream Catholic Church, revivalist Catholics could create a "cohesive moral community" within the pro-life movement (Cuneo 1989:105). They viewed the battle against abortion as a final holdout against the liberal direction of Canadian Catholicism, and they bitterly resented the reluctance of the hierarchy of the Canadian Catholic Church to become involved in the politics of the abortion conflict. (In this regard, the Canadian Catholic Church differs from the Catholic Church in the United States, which has been much more active in the abortion conflict.) As revivalist Catholics became increasingly upset by the lack of support for the movement exhibited by the Canadian bishops, they helped to extend the family heritage frame for the abortion issue at the expense of the civil rights frame (Cuneo 1989:84–85).

Pro-Life Activists in the United States

In the United States, there has also been diversity and change over time in the anti-abortion movement. Early anti-abortion activists were mostly Catholics, some political liberals. In California, Luker (1984:135) found that many of the first anti-abortion activists were Catholic male professionals such as doctors or social workers who came into contact with pregnant women and the abortion issue through their work. In a study of the abortion conflict in Fargo, North Dakota, Faye Ginsburg (1989) also found that early anti-abortion activists tended to be male professionals. Like the civil rights activists in Cuneo's study, these people based their opposition to abortion on a belief in the sacredness of innocent human life and assumed that others in the public would agree with them when informed about the issue (Ginsburg 1989:130).

After the Supreme Court legalized abortion in 1973 with its *Roe v. Wade* ruling, a new type of recruit came into the anti-abortion movement (Luker 1984). The newcomers were mostly housewives who had not been politically active in the past but who were jolted into action by the Supreme Court decision. Like Cuneo's family heritage activists, these pro-life women share a worldview based on gender and family concerns. First of all, they believe that the sexes are intrinsically different, that women are naturally more suited to child rearing and homemaking than men, who are more suited to the public world (Luker 1984:159). These women recognize that many women work outside the home, and almost all of them agree that women should receive equal pay for equal work. However, they regard motherhood as a full-time job and do not believe mothers should work outside the home (Luker 1984:161). Not all pro-life activists feel this way, but they do explicitly connect abortion to motherhood and gender identity. Women who advocate abortion or have abortions are seen as lacking in femininity, whereas those who accept pregnancy, even if unwanted, are perceived as nurturant and "truly" female (Ginsburg 1989:110).

The value of children and the sanctity of parent-child relations are central concerns for many abortion opponents. Many pro-life activists feel stigmatized because they have large families and find themselves at odds with the dominant view that the number and timing of children should be carefully planned. In general, they feel that the society is anti-child. As one person said:

> [I]t doesn't seem to me that [children are] looked on as positively as they used to be. People look down on someone who wants to have more than two kids. Kids are looked on as a burden, [as] work. And they are. [People aren't] looking at the fun side of it and the nice side of it. (Luker 1984:170)

Many pro-lifers are highly offended by the notion of "recreational" sex. They see sex as "literally sacred" because it has the potential of creating new life (Luker 1984:165). Many pro-lifers do not use "artificial" contraceptives, not simply because they are Catholic—many Catholics do use contraceptives despite Church teachings—but because contraceptives foreclose the possibility of conception. The "natural family planning" method, based on calculation of fertility periods, is popular with pro-lifers precisely because it is not 100 percent reliable (Luker 1984:167–68). From the pro-life perspective, parenthood is a natural role and not one that should require a great deal of planning.

Teenage sexuality is of particular concern to pro-lifers, both because unmarried teenagers are using sex for enjoyment without being prepared for responsible parenthood and because the availability of contraceptives and abortion often leaves parents out, as a pro-life woman laments:

 [F]amily planning is sexual education. It's planned downtown with Planned Parenthood, it's not planned with the parents. So [under] the laws which exist now, the children get contraceptives without parental consent. What it's doing is [creating] a gap in family relationships. And the home and the family . . . should be the primary source of moral values. Well, if some parents don't take responsibility, then I think it's the responsibility of education to encourage parents to do it, rather than take it away from them—which is what has happened. (Luker 1984:174)

Another activist (quoted in Staggenborg 1987) links abortion to the immorality of sex for pleasure outside marriage and the lack of parental influence on children:

[Abortion] is such an important issue because it shows that the country is so *selfish*. Abortion is necessary when a certain life-style is adopted—a free and easy life-style that allows people to have sex without responsibility—the Playboy philosophy. This is symptomatic of the whole thing—abortion is being used as a backup contraceptive. . . . [By allowing teenagers access to contraceptives and abortion] we're destroying kids, destroying marriage, and damaging the fiber of this society. . . . I've always been against abortion, but the Supreme Court decision was a real shock to me. . . . I looked around for different groups in the pro-life movement [after the court decision]. (P. 790)

In short, many activists who joined the U.S. pro-life movement after abortion was legalized by the Supreme Court in 1973 were people with strong concerns about gender and family that they linked to abortion as either a cause or symbol of broader problems. However, these activists are not all antifeminists; many express support for positions such as equal pay for women. Donald Granberg's survey of the National Right to Life Committee, which is considered a "mainstream" pro-life organization, reflects the views of these constituents.

On the left of the mainstream pro-life movement, some, particularly liberal Catholics, have attempted to form "progressive" pro-life groups. Pro-Lifers for Survival, which opposes nuclear arms as well as abortion, and Feminists for Life are two organizations formed by women who consider themselves feminists (Paige 1983:67–68). These activists stress social justice and collective responsibility rather than individual rights. Within the Catholic Church, some bishops, such as the late Joseph Cardinal Bernardin, have advocated a progressive "seamless garment" pro-life position, in which opposition to abortion is linked to antinuclear, antipoverty, and other pro-life efforts. The socially progressive, evangelical Christian publication *Sojourners* also links its anti-abortion position to its concerns with racism and poverty (Blanchard 1994:39).

The New Christian Right

Many of these liberal voices within the pro-life camp have been drowned out by those of the cultural and religious fundamentalists who have come to dominate the anti-abortion movement since the late 1970s. The fundamentalists include both Catholics and Protestants who share a concern with church dogma and a commitment to the traditional authority of the father in the home (Blanchard 1994:41–45). Since World War II, fundamentalist and evangelical churches have grown enormously in the United States, whereas liberal and mainline Protestant churches have lost members (Wuthnow 1986–87:228). Through the efforts of the political New Right, these constituents were mobilized politically in the 1970s into what analysts have called the New Christian Right (see Liebman and Wuthnow 1983). Abortion has been one of the key issues used to mobilize these conservative Christians for political action.

Conservative Christians have long shared traditional values with regard to gender and family; to maintain their communities, they need to socialize their children to accept these beliefs. Abortion is a central issue for conservative Christians not only because of their religious beliefs against the practice, but also because of its effect on their ability to transmit parental values to children:

> Abortion necessarily involves sex, and premarital teenage sex at that, aside from the obvious Pro-Choice and Pro-Life debate on the rights of the fetus and the rights of the mother. Thus it hits the conservative Christian nerve, Catholic and Protestant alike, at its most exposed spot, for everything that the [New Christian Right] and many other conservative Christians think has gone awry in the United States, the sexual revolution, the rebellion of youth, the redefinition of sex roles, the undermining of marriage, rampant

immorality, hedonism, irreligion, venereal disease, and welfare mothers come together in female, teenage, premarital sexual intercourse. To opponents, abortion is a license that invites all these evils, and lets the culprits off the hook, at the taxpayers' expense. (Oberschall 1993:361)

If the schools, the mass media, and other institutions uphold the parents' values, the task of socialization is easier (Oberschall 1993:375). But if teachers, peers, and others expose children to alternative values and behaviors, the culture of a religious community is indeed threatened. In fighting against the influence of values and behaviors associated with abortion, the New Christian Right is not only fighting "subversive influences emanating from New York and San Francisco" but also providing "protection against internal change" (p. 380).

For the most active constituency in the anti-abortion movement, then, concerns about family and gender are closely linked to the issue of abortion. Abortion is seen as both a symbol and a cause of changes such as unstable marriage, the declining influence of parents over children's values, and immoral sexual behavior. Other constituents of the pro-life movement who are not conservative Christians also link abortion to family and gender issues, but they do not share the entire New Christian Right agenda. Some pro-lifers, notably liberal Catholics, are not particularly concerned about gender and family issues but simply oppose abortion out of the religious belief that the practice is wrong. Some politically liberal activists would like to link the issue of abortion to social justice issues such as poverty and racism or to other matters of "life," such as nuclear proliferation. Thus there is a diversity of views within the anti-abortion movement, but a conservative "pro-family" frame is publicly dominant because of the influence of its adherents within the movement.

Abortion Rights Perspectives

Like the anti-abortion movement, the abortion rights movement has always been diverse. In the 1960s, a movement to reform the U.S. abortion laws gathered support from long-time supporters of family planning, population control, and civil liberties as well as from the emerging feminist movement. The leaders of the small "abortion movement" tended to be people with years of experience in established organizations, such as Planned Parenthood and the Democratic Party.

Many of the early abortion rights activists saw abortion as an extension of contraception, which enjoyed widespread public acceptance. To build on that acceptance, they tried not to threaten audiences in debating the issue. For example, the leader of an early abortion law repeal organization in Illinois was careful about how she presented herself at speaking engagements in the 1960s and early 1970s: "I always tried to start out by saying something about myself—like, 'I have three children, I've been married to the same man for 20 years, and I've never had an abortion'" (quoted in Staggenborg 1991:32). Some early activists were surprised that the reforms they advocated provoked controversy:

> The YMCA and the [American Medical Association] auxiliary and the [American Association of University Women] came out early with pro-choice statements. They were very modest. They were so rational that we thought there would be no problem getting people to accept it. It was a shock to see what people would do, to find out how angry they were. We thought we were trying to be moderate. (Quoted in Ginsburg 1989:68)

Women's Liberation

Women's liberationists, on the other hand, saw the abortion issue as something much more radical. As young women began to meet in the small groups that made up the younger branch of the women's movement, they developed the idea that "the personal is political." That is, they talked about issues such as sexuality, women's health, and gender and family relations that were previously considered private and analyzed them as political issues. One important goal of feminist writing and discussion was to provide women with information about their bodies that would empower them to find out more and to take charge of their lives. Abortion was critical to the movement because it is a concrete issue that affects personal lives and the ability of women to control their bodies and their sexuality.

Radical young feminists held "speak-outs" in which women talked publicly and often movingly about abortion and other personal experiences such as rape. In contrast to more mainstream reformers, who argued for legal abortion to avoid the tragedies associated with illegal abortion (see Condit 1990), these feminists began calling for "abortion on demand" as a condition of women's liberation.

Although more pragmatic abortion reformers saw this type of rhetoric as detrimental to the cause, radical young feminists wanted to challenge existing institutions such as marriage and the family and to create a new consciousness regarding women. As a feminist activist in the 1960s later explained:

I think we felt that "abortion on demand" was the thing that would appeal to the most people, most women. . . . [I]n the course of their lives, every single woman has probably had a chance or thought about an abortion. . . . We felt that that demand would bring more people in. . . . And part of it was just breaking out. Just changing something, breaking out from things. The most far-out thing was the one that you wanted to advocate because you felt that people would say, "You're right," you know, and break out— because everyone was feeling so repressed. (Quoted in Staggenborg 1991:45)

From the perspective of feminists in the radical branch of the women's movement in the 1960s, abortion was part of the far-reaching changes they were advocating. But it was precisely the type of change feared by cultural conservatives.

Individual Choice

Whereas the approach of the women's liberationists seemed appropriate in the context of the social movements of the 1960s, the abortion rights movement had to defend its position throughout the changing political climate of subsequent decades. Thus, abortion rights groups such as the National Abortion Rights Action League (NARAL) worked hard to frame the abortion issue in a way that builds on public opinion and dominant American values. Although the notion of abortion as a "women's right" is at odds with the ideology of Christian conservatives, who would stress responsibility to family and community over individual rights, it is in line with the dominant American focus on individual rights (see Morton 1992). Within the U.S. legal system, it is necessary to use "rights discourse" to gain power because "judicial interpretation of constitutional rights provides the primary vehicle for advancing the interests of the individual citizen as balanced against the interests of the state" (Bortner 1990:99). Indeed, abortion was legalized based on the "right to privacy" that the U.S. Supreme Court applied to cases involving contraception and abortion.

Adoption of the "pro-choice" label was also important in the effort to make abortion rights a mainstream issue. Many people who would never call themselves "pro-abortion" agree that abortion should be a matter of individual choice. After the Supreme Court legalized abortion in 1973, a number of churches and synagogues joined together in an organization called the Religious Coalition for Abortion Rights (RCAR) and adopted the position that abortion can be a moral choice in some circumstances. Recently, the organization changed its name to the Religious Coalition for

Reproductive Choice to further emphasize its commitment to "women's health and reproductive choices" (Fried 1994:7).

In the late 1980s and 1990s, pro-choice groups such as NARAL have used sophisticated political technologies—such as polls, media advisers, and focus groups—to help package the pro-choice message. One particularly effective theme that came out of focus group research is NARAL's "Who decides?" slogan, which asks whether it should be the government or women and their families who decide who should have an abortion. According to NARAL president Kate Michelman, this theme was adopted in 1989 shortly after she observed a focus group through a one-way mirror. She heard a middle-aged woman say, "You know, the real question is, who decides?" In Michelman's view the slogan "mainstreamed the issue" and "made being anti-choice anti-American" (Matlack 1991:630). NARAL used the slogan, along with its Statue of Liberty logo, on bumper stickers, posters, and television spots. The organization's anti-government-interference, pro-choice message proved to have strong public appeal in some high-profile political contests, including the 1989 New Jersey and Virginia gubernatorial races, in which pro-choice Democrats were elected by narrow margins.

NARAL has also used polling data and focus group research to shape its own agenda. In response to findings that most Americans dislike the rhetoric of the abortion debate and its excessive focus on the single issue of abortion, NARAL in 1992 released its new "comprehensive pro-choice agenda," which includes sex education, contraceptive research, and prenatal care in addition to abortion rights (Warner 1993:24). To reflect this broader focus, the organization also changed its name to the National Abortion and Reproductive Rights Action League (retaining the use of its familiar acronym, NARAL).

Family Values

Although the individual choice and anti-government-interference frame has been very successful in helping the pro-choice movement appeal to mainstream Americans, it is not the only perspective on abortion among feminists. Some feminists, like the temperance and women's peace activists before them, use maternalist rhetoric to connect with traditional female culture and distance themselves from 1960s-style radical feminism. In Fargo, North Dakota, for example, local pro-choice activists subscribe to what they call "midwestern feminism," a version of "difference" feminism that emphasizes women's importance in sustaining the values of caring and nurturance. Some see their concerns as different from those emphasized by feminists elsewhere. For example, one midwestern feminist said:

> I don't really even read Ms. magazine anymore. It just doesn't talk about my life or other women in Fargo. You know, we still have potlucks here. We're worried about our community, raising decent kids, our marriages, getting old with or without a man. These are basic priorities that we all have to work together on. (Quoted in Ginsburg 1989:125)

These feminists do not sound very different from their opponents on the abortion issue when they talk of female caregiving and nurturance and the importance of society's "responsibility for caring for its children" (p. 125). They see legal abortion as one means of supporting family life, as a pro-choice activist explained:

> I think it's easy for them [opponents] to stereotype us as having values very different from theirs and that's not the case at all. Many of the people who get abortions have values very similar to the antiabortion people. The right-to-life people don't know how deeply I care for my own family. . . . The perspective that abortion is "destroying the family" is a very, very narrow one. In my experience, people who have made the choice to have an abortion made it because they want a strong family. How bringing an unwanted child into a family strengthens it is something I have never been able to understand. (Quoted in Ginsburg 1989:154)

A pro-family, pro-choice position has also been articulated by others, such as Jerry Muller in "The Conservative Case for Abortion" (1995). Muller notes that the abortion debate is typically framed as the "right to choose" versus the "right to life"; but a third, typically overlooked, position "favors abortion as the right choice to promote healthy family life under certain circumstances" (Muller 1995:27). This is essentially a conservative, pro-family position that is associated with middle-class values in modern society:

> The pro-life movement is at odds with the assumptions of middle-class family formation. These families believe that the bearing and rearing of children is not an inexorable fate but a voluntary vocation, and that, like any other vocation, it is to be pursued methodically using the most effective means available. Such a conception of the family includes planning when children are to be born and how many are to be born. It seeks to increase the chances of successfully socializing and educating children to help them find fulfilling work and spiritual lives. The number of children is kept low in part because the amount of parental time and resources devoted to raising them is expected to be high. (Muller 1995:28)

In this perspective, people who value families may still consider abortion to be the best choice—for example, unmarried mothers unprepared to care for a child and parents whose children would be born with severe genetic defects, causing suffering to themselves and their families. Thus, the concern is not so much for individual rights, but for the collective good of the family.

Reproductive Rights

On the political left, advocates of legal abortion have also tried to focus on collective responsibilities rather than on individual rights alone. Within the pro-choice movement, feminists with roots in the radical branch of the women's movement have developed a "reproductive rights" approach (see Petchesky 1984; Staggenborg 1991). This feminist perspective is concerned with both the individual woman's "right" to control her body and the societal conditions that would make having a child a real choice for women, including access to health care, jobs, child care, and education. Feminists working in this branch of the pro-choice movement have been particularly concerned with issues related to social class, such as access to funding for abortions, and issues that affect minority women, such as sterilization abuse.

Although feminists generally agree that individual women have a "right" to choose abortion, some recognize that simply having the right is inadequate. As Rosalind Petchesky (1989) wrote in response to NARAL's strategy, "The issue of 'who decides' is important. But being able to 'decide' will not necessarily get a woman an abortion, much less improve the conditions of her life." Pressing social problems such as poverty, AIDS, and race and sex discrimination "are not and will not be solvable through 'individual choice'" but, rather, require collective solutions (Petchesky 1989:10). Although a "rights" discourse has benefited women, it is inadequate because it does not address the "social and economic conditions that necessitate the right to abort and minimize the opportunity to meaningfully parent" (Bortner 1990:107).

Common Concerns

Both the pro-life movement and the pro-choice movement consist of diverse constituencies. But looking at the range of perspectives, we can detect some common concerns related to family and gender. With regard to sexuality, pro-life women share with pro-choice feminists a concern

about the sexual exploitation of women. For example, feminists and social conservatives have sometimes joined forces on the issue of pornography (see Segal and McIntosh 1992; Vance 1984). Furthermore, feminists
and some pro-lifers are searching for "alternative modes of heterosexual
relationships" (Joffe 1986–87:210–11). Feminists seek sexual freedom
without sexual exploitation, and social conservatives typically wish to
confine sex to marriage. Both, however, are struggling with the changing
sexual norms and behaviors of the twentieth century.

There are also some common concerns about family life. Feminists
have tried to alter gender relations within families so that men and
women are more equal, but they have also been concerned about preserv-
ing and extending women's values, such as caring and nurturance, into
realms, such as the workplace, that have traditionally been dominated by
competitive, masculine values. Pro-life women sometimes wish to preserve traditional gender roles in the family, but they too care about nurturance as a feminine value. In addition, pro-life and pro-choice activists
alike often interpret their abortion positions as means of strengthening
family life.

Some feminists and pro-lifers also share concern with community and
collective responsibility. Pro-lifers typically see abortion as a disavowal
of family and community responsibilities in favor of individual rights.
Many feminists, however, would like to see more collective responsibility
for children and better conditions for men and women to freely choose
parenthood. In both views, the collective good is greater than the interests of individuals.

In addition to sharing some common concerns, some activists on opposite sides of the abortion issue are willing to respect one another's humanity. In Fargo, North Dakota, for example, most local activists on both
sides are women who live in the same neighborhoods and sometimes see
one another in settings such as PTA meetings, the YWCA, and voluntary
organizations (Ginsburg 1989). A pro-choice activist describes her relationship with a pro-life woman with whom she works on the board of a
community service organization:

> I remember when I met Myra and I was really enjoying her and when I
> found out her position [on abortion] I was really surprised, you know, but
> I was able to say, OK, I understand. I respect Myra's position and she re-
> spects mine and neither of us have any fantasies about changing the other.
> And I think we both recognize that it's a very complex and difficult issue.
> I find with Myra that there is unity on other values, or at least nothing that
> leads to conflict. (Quoted in Ginsburg 1989:114)

Similarly, a pro-life activist who does "sidewalk counseling" at the local abortion clinic wrote a note to one of the counselors at the clinic after the latter had written an article in the newspaper about her experience with sexual assault:

> After walking out in front of the clinic for two months and seeing and praying for you, I felt a closeness in the spirit. I've had a longing to talk with you but that is impossible under the circumstances. I lift you before the Lord daily. We also live in the same neighborhood, so there is a closeness there. (Quoted in Ginsburg 1989:112)

Most Fargo pro-choice and pro-life activists at the time of the Ginsburg study were moderates. Pro-life activists were typically very constrained in their activities. In sidewalk counseling at the abortion clinic, for example, they walked and prayed, gave out literature, and engaged women in conversation when possible, but they did not scream at clinic clients or confront them physically. Their activism was very much influenced by their conception of womanhood as loving and caring; they disdained strident demonstrations as unfeminine and tried to show their nurturant qualities through their actions (Ginsburg 1989:99–100). Similarly, the tactics of local pro-choice activists were influenced by their "midwestern feminism." As a Fargo woman who was active in 1976 in defending the abortion clinic there explained:

> We are feminists, but we are not rabble-rousing bra burners. We named the group the Baker's Center for Women because we are also feminine and the idea of baking bread is very woman oriented. It also has a spiritual meaning in the sense of breaking bread together, a communion of people with similar needs. (Quoted in Ginsburg 1989:79)

As this quotation illustrates, even women who consider themselves feminists are influenced by stereotypes of the women's movement like the media-constructed image of feminists as "bra burners." Nevertheless, local feminists can be particularly effective when they fit their goals with the local culture and make "symbolic connections with home, family, and religion" (Quoted in Ginsburg 1989:79).

Polarization in the Abortion Conflict

Despite the common concerns of pro-life and pro-choice activists, the two sides have become polarized. Their positions have become simplified as the opposing movements have responded to one another and to new events in the abortion battle and as particular constituents have come to dominate each movement, pushing their tactics and ideologies. The mass media have been important in this process because they generally favor coverage of conflict and simplified positions over compromise and complicated views (see Gans 1979; Gitlin 1980).

Thus opposition to abortion has increasingly become associated with right-wing, antifeminist politics; support for abortion has become a requisite of feminist allegiance. Women who oppose abortion have difficulty fitting into liberal and feminist circles if they are so inclined. Pro-life women report being forced into an antifeminist mold by virtue of their views on abortion. For example, a pro-life delegate to the White House Conference on Families in 1980 commented, "I strongly believe in equal opportunity for women. And I didn't like being labeled at this White House Conference that I was against all these rights for women just because I took this stand on abortion" (Ginsburg 1989:83–84).

Even in Fargo, North Dakota, where pro-choice and pro-life activists shared many values, polarization occurred. In 1983, following a Supreme Court ruling that essentially reaffirmed the 1973 legalization of abortion in *Roe v. Wade*, a new anti-abortion group called Save-a-Baby formed, drawing its constituency primarily from the conservative Christian population. The group employed confrontational tactics very different from those of the older LIFE (Life Is for Everyone) Coalition in Fargo:

> In contrast to the relatively quiet, moderate tactics of LIFE, the Save-a-Baby activists stopped just short of violence in their weekly demonstrations. They gathered outside the clinic in groups as large as thirty and screamed at women entering the building not to kill their babies, displaying large signs with Biblical quotes and pictures of whole and mutilated fetuses. They blocked traffic, followed patients leaving the facility, and even picketed the homes of the clinic's administrator and physician, carrying signs with slogans likening them to Hitler. (Ginsburg 1989:115)

Although Save-a-Baby consisted of only about 50 activists compared to the 1,300 members of LIFE Coalition, the new group attracted a great deal of media attention as a result of its confrontational tactics. In 1984, the ABC news program *20/20* did a segment on the Fargo abortion conflict, which featured Save-a-Baby activists and completely ignored the more moderate pro-life activists. The radical anti-abortionists, although not representative of the larger movement in Fargo, made for more dramatic television than did the moderates. Although they were privately very upset with this development, the moderates did not try to distinguish themselves publicly from the radicals, thereby adding to the public perception of the extremism of the movement (Ginsburg 1989:119).

Extremism in the anti-abortion movement became even more pronounced after Operation Rescue began massive blockades of abortion clinics in 1988. A recent study of a feminist clinic in a southeastern U.S. city (Simonds 1996) provides a stark contrast to Ginsburg's earlier study of Fargo, North Dakota. When Operation Rescue assaulted the clinic, its "workers were plunged into an ordeal they described as nightmarish, hellish, and extremely anxiety producing" (Simonds 1996:107). During the siege and in subsequent smaller-scale demonstrations, clinic workers were subjected to harsh verbal assaults on a daily basis. They feared for their own safety and that of the women seeking abortions at the clinic (particularly after the murders of several doctors and staff that took place at abortion clinics in the early 1990s). Clinic staff witnessed the hostility of anti-abortion demonstrators toward women as they "screamed at and aggressively surrounded clients and attempted to block their way" (Simonds 1996:113). As a result of their experience with such protests, clinic workers felt a great deal of anger and even hatred toward their opponents. In this polarized situation, there was no room for moderation and mutual understanding between opponents.

Moderates also became less visible in the Canadian anti-abortion movement (Cuneo 1989). As the Canadian abortion rate escalated and the feminist movement flourished, grassroots anti-abortion activists became increasingly frustrated. They began to challenge their movement's civil rights presentation, which opposed abortion as a matter of science and human rights, and introduced themes of family and religion. The family heritage activists distrusted female civil rights leaders who had careers; as a result, in the late seventies two professional women who were the executive directors of an anti-abortion organization resigned in succession (Cuneo 1989:23). Because of these developments, civil rights activists became more and more peripheral within the Canadian anti-abortion movement. Many began to feel like outsiders, despite their opposition to abortion, because they did not share the religious beliefs or cultural concerns of family heritage and revivalist Catholic activists.

Whereas the Canadian civil rights activists were willing to compromise and to tone down their rhetoric in the hope that they might have a real impact, the newer activists were unwilling to alter their purist stance. For revivalist Catholics, the movement provided a home outside the Church, and expression of their beliefs was more important than instrumental results (Cuneo 1989). The nonconfrontational and compromising stance of the civil rights activists was closer to the values of the Canadian public, but the movement became increasingly conducive to radical views. This is a prime example of how the internal dynamics of a social movement can determine which perspectives prevail in public presentations of an issue.

Within the pro-choice movement, a single-issue, individual rights perspective has dominated. Feminist reproductive rights activists have tried to alter this frame by discussing abortion as part of a multi-issue agenda that includes sterilization abuse as well as other issues. After passage in 1976 of the federal Hyde Amendment banning Medicaid funding of abortions, reproductive rights groups also tried to get larger pro-choice groups like NARAL to focus on regaining public funding for poor women. In the political climate of the late 1970s and 1980s, however, feminists failed to alter the single-issue abortion rights agenda (see Staggenborg 1991).

Reproductive rights activists did not fail because the larger pro-choice movement lacked sympathetic feminists but because the successful attacks of the anti-abortion movement made it difficult for groups such as NARAL to broaden their focus. The New Right was becoming a political force, and in 1980 an avowedly anti-abortion president, Ronald Reagan, was elected. Pro-choice groups were desperately trying to defend existing abortion rights; they did not feel they could broaden the pro-choice agenda or even regain Medicaid funding.

When reproductive rights groups tried to influence other groups to adopt their multi-issue approach, they sometimes created conflict within the movement. For example, a Chicago reproductive rights group called Women Organized for Reproductive Choice (WORC) tried to influence a coalition group, the Illinois Pro-Choice Alliance, to take a multi-issue approach and to focus on class issues associated with abortion. But WORC mostly created resentment, as a participant in the alliance commented in an interview:

> It was really hard to take a group like WORC coming in and talking like we didn't care about sterilization abuse, like we didn't care about poor women. Other people in the coalition really resented their holier-than-thou attitude. It's just not true that the rest of us don't care about poor women or other issues. But it was like, first things first; right now we're fighting this battle. (Quoted in Staggenborg 1991:120)

Even within a movement, then, misunderstandings and differences in frames and strategies make it hard for some perspectives to be heard.

In the 1990s, the political climate has been more conducive to a multi-issue pro-choice agenda. Although the political right is still intent on outlawing abortion, it has not succeeded in doing so through the courts or legislatures. NARAL has adopted a multi-issue reproductive rights approach because it seemed politically advisable to do so, but it is not clear how radical the group's perspective will be. The Religious Coalition for Reproductive Choice, which has a Women of Color Partnership Program, is also trying to advance a multi-issue reproductive rights agenda that addresses class and race issues (Fried 1994). It remains to be seen, however, whether multi-issue, feminist visions of family and community will be developed as a positive alternative to the antifeminist views promoted by anti-abortionists.

Conclusion

The spread of legal abortion in the twentieth century coincides with numerous social changes affecting family and gender relations, such as rising divorce rates, the entry of women into the labor force, and increases in premarital sex. Men and women, feminists and antifeminists alike, are trying to come to terms with these changes, and abortion is important to their struggles, both symbolically and practically.

As feminists contend, abortion helps women take control of their lives. With safe and legal abortion available as a backup to failed contraception, women can engage in sexual relations without fear of unwanted pregnancy. Women can control the timing and number of children they will have, thereby allowing them more freedom for other endeavors such as education and careers. However, these benefits are not necessarily available to all women because there is no public funding of abortion in some countries, including the United States, and because educational and occupational opportunities are limited by class and race. Moreover, individual access to abortion does not address other feminist concerns regarding family life, such as the importance of men's participation in parenting and the need for social support of children.

For men and women who prefer a traditional family structure—in which the man is the authority, the woman's priority is home and children, and the children are obedient to their parents—abortion represents a real threat. They believe that women who have other choices will have a hard time choosing to refrain from sex outside of marriage and to devote themselves to their families rather than careers. And, for parents who are trying to pass traditional family values on to their children, it is difficult to compete with other sources of influence, such as the schools and the mass media. When abortion and contraception are available to teenagers, parents may lose their ability to control their children's sex lives.

The ongoing conflict over abortion raises critical questions for heterogeneous societies: Is it possible for a diverse society to accommodate the concerns of all its citizens? Can we help social conservatives safeguard their lifestyles and values for their children at the same time that we protect women's rights and permit men and women—and boys and girls— to adopt new gender roles? Or does the fight over abortion symbolize an inevitable "culture war"? If so, which side will win? Given the social changes that have occurred and the public's moderate views on abortion, perhaps a "conservative middle-class" position, one that accepts abortion as a pro-family measure, is most likely to prevail.

6

The Battle over
Gay and Lesbian Rights

If any issue rivals abortion in terms of the intensity of conflict that it has provoked, it is homosexuality. While gay and lesbian rights movements have tried to "normalize" same-sex relations and gain civil rights for their constituents, opponents have struggled to maintain the idea that homosexuality and bisexuality are socially deviant. Why is there so much conflict over this issue? Why do some people care about what other people do in their private relationships? By looking at the conflict in the context of changes in family and gender relations, we can begin to understand some of the intensity of the opposition to same-sex sexuality and bisexuality. We can also see that the gay and lesbian rights movement presents a real challenge to traditional ideas about gender and family.

Same-Sex Relationships and Social Change

Throughout history and across cultures, many forms of same-sex relations have existed, but there has not always been a "homosexual" identity that could provide the basis for a social movement. Gay and lesbian identities came with the development of capitalism and the shift from rural to urban society (Adam 1995; D'Emilio 1993; Katz 1995). With this transformation, people became mobile wage earners, and individuals gained new freedom from obligatory ties to family and community. This is not to say that ties to family and community declined in urban societies; family historians have provided extensive documentation of their ongoing importance, particularly to working-class and immigrant families (see Hareven 1987). Nevertheless, in urban industrial societies, individuals had more freedom to live outside nuclear family arrangements if they so desired, and cities offered the possibility of anonymity and privacy. With the development of modern society, the primary meaning of sexuality changed as well: from reproduction within families to emotional intimacy and physical pleasure for individuals (D'Emilio and Freedman 1988).

The Rise of Nonreproductive Sexuality

In colonial American society, the norm of marital sexuality was enforced by communities through the churches and through laws. Although prenuptial pregnancy rates were high in some regions at certain times, couples who conceived before marriage were typically fined and whipped and, of course, forced to marry (D'Emilio and Freedman 1988:22). Deviance from marital, reproductive sexuality was severely punished in the colonies. Adulterers were often punished by fines "along with public whippings or the wearing of the letters AD on a garment or burned into the forehead" (p. 28). Nonprocreative or "unnatural" sexual acts, including sodomy and bestiality, carried the death penalty. Although executions were rare, offenders were often severely whipped, burned with a hot iron, or banished (p. 30). To enforce the norms of marital, reproductive sexuality, neighbors kept a close watch on one another and testified against offenders in court. Norms and behavior varied with class and race however; for example, "southern white men of the planter class enjoyed extreme sexual privilege" as long as they had their sex "discreetly with poor white or black women" (p. 95).

Community control over sexuality began to break down as geographical mobility increased and larger towns developed. In the growing cities and in the expanding West, opportunities increased for nonmarital sexuality, including same-sex relations. Wage-earning men found anonymity in the city and could bring other men to their rooms in urban boardinghouses (D'Emilio and Freedman 1988:123). In the nineteenth century, the military, prisons, and the wide open spaces of the West provided young single men with opportunities for same-sex relations.

Women had fewer opportunities, but working-class women sometimes "passed" as men so that they could earn wages and marry other women (D'Emilio and Freedman 1988:124). Among middle-class women, particularly those who attended female colleges in the nineteenth century, opportunities arose for intensely romantic friendships between women. Because female sexuality was closely linked to reproduction at that time, erotic friendships between women were to some extent acceptable until "the separation of sexuality and reproduction made Americans more conscious of the erotic element of these friendships" (p. 126).

The breakdown of the "procreative standard" of sexual normality also paved the way for the emergence of an opposition between "homosexuality" and "heterosexuality" (Katz 1995:19–20). In the late nineteenth century, when the terms were first used to refer to same-sex and different-sex attraction, both "homo" and "hetero" referred to abnormal deviations from procreative, marital intercourse. Only when the norm of procreative sexuality had weakened sufficiently did heterosexuality became "normal sexuality" (Katz 1995:92).

Gay and Lesbian Subcultures

By the early twentieth century, substantial homosexual subcultures had developed in the large cities of the Western world, including Paris, Berlin, and New York. These subcultures originated within the larger working-class culture that developed in urban areas as young men and women took part in the amusements and freedoms of urban life. Men had more freedom than women, and gay male subcultures were more extensive than lesbian subcultures in the early twentieth century. However, single working women also frequented dance halls, movies, and other amusements (Peiss 1986). By the second decade of the twentieth century, women also went to saloons, particularly those that offered food as well as drink, even though saloons were considered dangerous for unescorted women (Peiss 1986:28). Thus, in the 1920s, working-class lesbians began to develop a lesbian subculture around bars (Faderman 1991:79–80).

During the 1920s, Prohibition led to an expansion of nightclubs and speakeasies that sold illegal liquor. These establishments attracted middle-class men and women along with immigrants and working-class people. Reformers worried that the boundaries between respectable middle-class norms and dangerous working-class behavior were breaking down. In reality, middle-class city dwellers had been partaking of expanded commercial entertainment for over a generation, but the speakeasies allowed further experimentation with public norms of behavior (Chauncey 1994:307–308).

In this context, gay and lesbian subculture did not stand out so much and actually became quite fashionable. Drag balls, at which gay men dressed as women and some women wore tuxedos, became highly popular forms of public entertainment in cities such as New York, Chicago, and New Orleans in the 1920s and early 1930s. The balls were held in fashionable and large venues such as the Hotel Astor and Madison

Square Garden in New York and often attracted huge audiences. In the case of one highly successful ball in the 1920s, a Broadway gossip sheet reported "6000 Crowd Huge Hall as Queer Men and Women Dance" (Faderman 1991:66).

Public curiosity about homosexuality was enormous in the 1920s. Gay men came into demand as entertainers in New York nightclubs, starting a "pansy craze." Some pansy acts took to the road, and so the craze spread to other cities as well (Chauncey 1994:320–21). The pansy craze allowed middle-class club-goers to show their "sophistication" and distance themselves from the "narrow-minded" moral reformers responsible for Prohibition (p. 327). Similarly, bisexual experimentation or "lesbian chic" was "encouraged in some circles by a new value placed on the unconventional and daring" (Faderman 1991:64). Lesbianism became a popular theme in fiction in the 1920s, appearing in the novels of Ernest Hemingway among others, and sex with another woman became "the great adventure" (p. 67).

Even in the context of the sexual liberalism of the 1920s, however, there was great ambivalence about same-sex sexuality. Pansies were often ridiculed, betraying both "a fascination with the gay subculture and a nervousness about the questions its visibility raised regarding the inevitability of heterosexual arrangements" (Chauncey 1994:329). Although lesbianism was chic among sophisticated New Yorkers, many did not take it seriously (Faderman 1991:75). Genuine lesbian relationships were typically regarded as a threat to the ideal of companionate marriage between man and woman (p. 91). Both gay male and lesbian relationships faced resistance because they challenged existing gender relations.

Gay Men and Masculinity

The gay male world of the early twentieth century was very highly developed and, as historian George Chauncey (1994) describes in *Gay New York*, it was also fairly well integrated into male working-class culture. At first, there were no rigid distinctions between "homosexual" and "heterosexual" men. It was possible for a man to have sex with another man without taking on a "gay" identity.[1] Some men took on the role of the "fairy" and adopted effeminate mannerisms and flamboyant clothes that identified them as such. For example, fairies might wear green suits or red neckties and have plucked eyebrows or painted faces. Fairies mingled with other men in the saloons and streets where working-class men congregated. Many working-class men had sex with fairies as well as female prostitutes. However, there were important differences among working-class men based on race and ethnicity. For example, there was much greater tolerance of male homosexuality among Italian immigrants than among Jewish immigrants (Chauncey 1994:73).

Working-class men sometimes abused fairies, just as they did women, but they typically tolerated their presence and did not feel that their own manhood was threatened by the fairies. This was because fairies were considered a "third sex" or "intermediate type." By taking the role of women, fairies confirmed rather than threatened "normal" men's sense of masculinity; men who looked masculine were clearly men and not fairies, regardless of their sex partners (Chauncey 1994:56–57). Moreover, working-class men did not prove their manhood through heterosexual relations. In the dominant working-class ideology, men proved themselves by supporting their families.

For men who could not earn enough to support families or who deliberately rejected family obligations, the bachelor subculture of the city provided alternative means of showing manliness (Chauncey 1994:78–79). Working-class men proved their manliness in male arenas through rituals such as buying a round of drinks at the saloon or by engaging in contests of physical strength or skill such as boxing matches or games of pool. Although sexual conquests of women were also a sign of manliness,

> such prowess was significant not only as an indication of a man's ability to dominate women but also as evidence of his *relative* virility compared to other men's; manliness in this world was confirmed by other men and in relation to other men, not by women. (Chauncey 1994:80)

The situation of middle-class men was very different. Middle-class men in the late nineteenth and early twentieth centuries felt their manhood threatened because of the changing nature of their work and the challenges posed by both women and working-class and immigrant men. By the turn of the century, middle-class men typically worked at white-collar jobs in large, impersonal bureaucracies in which they could exert little autonomy or initiative. Women were entering the public sphere, demanding the vote and pushing reforms such as temperance on men. Working-class men, who were often immigrants, also challenged middle-class men's masculinity because they engaged in "manly" physical labor, while middle-class men were subject to being called "sissies."

Because they feared feminization, middle-class men had to define themselves in opposition to women. Many turned to sports such as prize-fighting, which became very popular as a spectator sport for middle-class men as they tried to maintain the boundaries between men's and women's spheres (Gorn 1986). The manly world of sports provided "temporary refuge from those forces which challenged their manhood, whether routined work, soulless corporations, aggressive women, smothering mothers, rich new industrialists, radical laborers, or swarthy foreigners" (Gorn 1986:194).

Homosexuality came to represent middle-class men's fears about loss of manhood. Thus, they saw having sex exclusively with women as proof of masculinity. The fairy was extremely threatening to middle-class men because "his effeminacy represented in extreme form the loss of manhood middle-class men most feared in themselves" (Chauncey 1994:115). The very existence of the fairy reminded men that gender was not immutable. Similarly, lesbian relationships also challenged ideas about the permanence of gender.

Lesbians and Changing Gender Roles

Because it was difficult for women to live independently, lesbian subculture was restricted and hard to find in the 1920s and 1930s. During the Depression, some working-class lesbian couples joined the hobo population, but middle-class women had little opportunity to live as lesbians if they wanted to retain their economic status (Faderman 1991:95). Significant numbers of lesbian bars did not appear in American cities until World War II, when more women came to urban areas to work (p. 107). In the 1940s and 1950s, lesbian bars thrived in many cities.

World War II was an important turning point not simply because the war created jobs for women, but because it "created a social atmosphere which encouraged women's independence" (Kennedy and Davis 1993:64). With many men away at war while women worked at their jobs, women were freer to socialize together. The war made all women more independent of men and their families, so that lesbians became "more like other women and less easy to identify" (Kennedy and Davis 1993:38). During the war, women were commonly seen together on the streets and many patronized bars. In addition, many women wore pants to work for the first time and commonly wore their work clothes in public. Lesbians who preferred pants could buy and wear them freely for the first time (p. 39).

Lesbians took advantage of the cultural transformations brought by the war to promote further changes in gender relations. A study of lesbians in Buffalo, New York (Kennedy and Davis 1993), describes how working-class lesbians created a community of women by socializing at bars in the 1940s and 1950s. Initially, this lesbian community was largely White and working-class because middle-class women were hesitant to go into bars and segregation kept many Black women away from bars in the 1940s. Black lesbians favored private house parties, which fit with the traditions of the larger Black community. But as segregation in the larger society began to break down in the 1950s, Black lesbians desegregated the bars. Some upwardly mobile women also began to go to lesbian bars, but they created their own culture distinct from that of working-class lesbians.

When working-class lesbians began to colonize bars in the 1940s, they significantly expanded the public space available to women. Unlike gay men, lesbians could not socialize in exposed areas such as parks because women were subject to harassment by men in such places. Although women had begun to participate in the leisure activities of the city in the early twentieth century, the culture created by these activities was "hetero-social," involving men and women (Peiss 1986). The streets were still dangerous places for unescorted women. Even though bars were traditionally male territory and lesbians, like gay men, faced the danger of arrest in them, bars were virtually the only place in which White working-class lesbians could meet. Many of these women lived with their families or in very small apartments. If they did live in apartments large enough for parties, they were subject to both harassment by neighbors and arrest (Kennedy and Davis 1993:30–31).

Bars were thus very important to the development of a working-class lesbian community. Through the bars, newcomers were able to locate others like themselves and to learn new gender roles. Within the bar culture, working-class lesbians typically took the role of either the "butch," who was masculine in appearance, or the "fem," who was traditionally feminine. Even though this "code of personal behavior for dress and mannerisms was modeled on heterosexual society, it was not simply imitative" (Kennedy and Davis 1993:167). Butches were not passing themselves off as men; they were developing a new way of being women. They developed a unique style of clothing, for example, which included tailor-made pants without a fly in the front rather than men's pants (p. 155). By appearing in public in such styles, butches risked trouble and challenged gender norms. Fems wore the styles of heterosexual women, such as high heels, but they also challenged existing norms by pairing up with butches.

From a contemporary perspective, the butch-fem model seems restrictive, and has been criticized by some feminists for its imitation of patriarchal gender roles. In the context of the 1940s and 1950s, however, the adoption of these roles was actually quite bold. The roles served as a "badge of identifiability among lesbians themselves and to the general public" (Kennedy and Davis 1993:153). Butch-fem roles allowed lesbians to recognize one another and they announced the possibility of love between women to the public. By being a butch or part of a butch-fem couple, lesbians in the 1940s and 1950s were claiming rather than denying an identity as a "homo" or "queer" (p. 169). This involved great risk and paved the way for women who could later claim a lesbian identity without taking on such roles.

Working-class lesbian culture in the 1940s and 1950s involved "prepolitical forms of resistance" that would provide one of the bases for the gay liberation movement of the 1960s (Kennedy and Davis 1993:150). The culture expanded the boundaries of acceptable female behavior by claiming new public spaces for socializing, introducing new fashions, and making new sexual relations possible. Amazingly, this expansion of women's culture occurred despite conservative reactions and efforts to protect the nuclear family.

The Backlash against Gays and Lesbians

A backlash against homosexuality first became evident during the Depression, when many men were thrown out of work and marriage rates plummeted as young people postponed marriage for financial reasons. Educators and clergy worried that this would lead to sexual transgressions (May 1988:39), and fears of loss of manhood became particularly pronounced. Because lower-paying female jobs were somewhat more available than male jobs during the Depression, families often had to rely on women's work to survive. Men lost status in their own eyes and in the eyes of their families. An unemployed father who talked to a *New York Daily News* reporter in 1932 asked, "What's wrong with me, that I can't protect my children?" A wife said of husbands, "They're not men anymore, if you know what I mean" (quoted in Mintz and Kellogg 1988:138–39).

To address anxieties about the family, in the 1930s some states passed laws to limit work by married women (see Ware 1982). They also passed laws cracking down on homosexuality. New York banned gay men and lesbians from gathering in any state-licensed public place and forbade the representation or discussion of homosexuality on stage. Hollywood prohibited the depiction of same-sex sexuality in its new film code, and state and local governments around the country outlawed female impersonation.

This backlash against gays and lesbians was clearly related to concerns raised by the Depression. Hostility toward lesbians in the 1930s was part of a more general increased hostility toward independent women (Faderman 1991:94). "Lesbians and gay men began to seem more dangerous in this context—as figures whose defiant perversity threatened to undermine the reproduction of normative gender and sexual arrangements already threatened by the upheavals of the thirties" (Chauncey 1994:354).

In some ways, middle-class men had a harder time swallowing the changes in gender and family relations associated with the Depression than did working-class men. Even before the Depression, industrial and unskilled workers regularly experienced periods of unemployment (Mintz and Kellogg 1988:135). Their families coped by relying on the earnings of women and children, taking in boarders, growing food in gardens, and using other survival strategies. The middle class, on the other hand, "had embraced a culture during the 1920s in which a nonworking wife, school-going children, and high household consumption were indicators of success, particularly that of the chief family breadwinner" (Cohen 1993:190).

Because middle-class men could no longer rely on breadwinning as a way of proving their manhood, many sought achievement in the home "as fathers and modest breadwinners (instead of as economic success stories), in the hope that by raising their sons to be successful men they could themselves achieve some masculine redemption" (Kimmel 1996:201). Advice books and popular writings urged fathers to take part in their sons' upbringing to instill masculine traits and prevent homosexuality. Mothers were faulted for being overly affectionate, but fathers could offset the dangers of mother love by instilling in their sons the attitudes, traits, and behaviors necessary to "real" men (Kimmel 1996:206). Homosexuality thus became symbolic of anxieties about gender at a time when it was increasingly difficult for men to succeed as breadwinners.

Both during the Depression and during World War II, there was a great deal of anxiety expressed about women's economic and sexual behavior, which seemed to be changing rapidly (May 1988:93). After the war, the family was looked to as a source of social stability and "nonmarital sexuality in all its forms became a national obsession" in the United States (May 1988:94). Anti-communist hysteria also reached new heights during the Cold War. In the early 1950s, Senator Joseph McCarthy and the House Un-American Activities Committee led the battle against domestic communism. During this period, many homosexuals, as well as alleged communists, were attacked by the committee and fired from their jobs (see D'Emilio 1983).

In the context of the Cold War, the family was seen as a defense against communism (May 1988). By adopting traditional gender roles and maintaining stable families, men and women could ward off threats to America. Homosexuality was thus linked to communism because it was seen as weakening the family and the country. In this view, "mannish" lesbians "mocked the ideals of marriage and motherhood" (D'Emilio 1983:49), while gay men, like communists, were failures of manhood (Adam 1995:61–62; Kimmel 1996:236).

Manhood, in the McCarthyite view, was tied to national self-esteem and involved toughness in standing up to the enemy. Domestic communists were seen as "soft spineless dupes of a foreign power, who were incapable of standing up for themselves" (Kimmel 1996:237). Gay men were similarly weak and represented the surrender of masculinity to female characteristics (Adam 1995:61–62). In the 1950s, men who became communists or homosexuals were seen as men who had failed to be men. In a time when it was not clear exactly what a real man was, it was easier to say what he was not; a real man was not a communist or a homosexual (Kimmel 1996:237).

During this era, men were still supposed to be breadwinners, but many middle-class men worked in dull jobs in large corporations where it was difficult to distinguish themselves. Male discontent with the life of the "gray flannel suit" was expressed in numerous discussions of the problem of "conformity" in middle-class male life such as *Look* magazine's 1958 article, "The American Male: Why Is He Afraid to Be Different?" (Ehrenreich 1983:30). In this story and others, the concern was expressed that American men might conform too much and thus become like communists. The answer to this problem, however, was not for men to leave their jobs and families for a more exciting life.

Although they feared conformity, middle-class men also feared failure as breadwinners and "the taint of homosexuality" that was likely to follow an attempt to escape male responsibilities (Ehrenreich 1983:24). Psychiatrist Dr. Abram Kardiner characterized the problem of male homosexuals:

> They cannot compete. They always surrender in the face of impending combat. This has nothing to do with their actual ability, for many of them have extraordinary talent. . . . These are men who are overwhelmed by the increasing demands to fulfill the specifications of masculinity. (Quoted in Ehrenreich 1983:24)

The fear of homosexuality outweighed the fear of conformity in middle-class men struggling to prove their manhood. Moreover, fathers had an important role in the family; they had to make their sons into men and prevent them from becoming homosexuals. By the 1950s, the middle-class norm of heterosexuality predominated in American culture (Katz 1995), and gays and lesbians were stigmatized and harassed as threats to the family, manhood, and national security.

However, "the targeting of gay men and women in the 1950s testified to the depth of changes that had occurred in the previous decade, for without them it is difficult to imagine the homosexual issue carrying much weight" (D'Emilio 1983:52). During the 1940s, the Kinsey reports had publicized the fact that homosexuality was widespread. World War II had provided large numbers of men and women with the opportunity to experience homosexual relations. Military conditions had thrown men into close contact with one another and "offered a protective covering that facilitated interaction among gay men" (D'Emilio 1983:26). Lesbians had been particularly prominent in the Women's Army Corps (WACS) and women outside the armed forces found themselves in all-female environments that created opportunities for lesbians to meet (pp. 27–29). Many gay men and lesbians built on networks formed during the war, settled in large cities, and helped to create an urban gay subculture that flourished despite legal persecution (p. 39).

The Gay and Lesbian Rights Movement

An organized and sustained gay and lesbian rights movement emerged in the United States with the founding of the Mattachine Society in Los Angeles in 1951. The founders of this organization saw gay men and lesbians as "an oppressed cultural minority" and wanted to build a large movement "capable of militancy" (D'Emilio 1983:63). As the organization grew, however, it attracted new leaders and a diverse constituency, including many who opposed militancy and even the view of gays and lesbians as an oppressed minority. Instead, they argued that "the sex variant is no different from anyone else except in the object of his sexual expression" and they urged gay men and lesbians not to develop a distinctive culture but to adopt a "pattern of behavior that is acceptable to society in general and compatible with [the] recognized institutions . . . of home, church, and state" (quoted in D'Emilio 1983:81). A lesbian group called the Daughters of Bilitis (DOB) that formed in 1955 took a similar stance, adopting as one of its objectives the advocacy of "a mode of behavior and dress acceptable to society" (quoted in Adam 1995:69–70).

There were strong disagreements within the "homophile" movement, as it was then called, over this conservative position. Some members of the Mattachine Society started a newsletter called *ONE*, which advocated a more radical view of gay pride and gained a national circulation. For the most part, however, the movement adopted a nonconfrontational stance appropriate to the 1950s, when gays and lesbians were being persecuted and were still struggling with internalized views of themselves shaped by the dominant culture's distaste for homosexuality (D'Emilio 1983:91). The leading strategy of the movement was "to stress the common humanity of homosexuals and heterosexuals and keep sexuality as such private" (Adam 1995:69).

This perspective changed in the 1960s, when a wave of new social movements mobilized to fight for such causes as civil rights, women's rights, environmentalism, and an end to the Vietnam War. In this context, it seemed possible to bring about change through militant collective action. The women's movement was challenging traditional gender roles, making it easier for gays and lesbians to do so as well. Moreover, working-class lesbians had already established a culture of defiance against traditional gender roles by presenting themselves openly as butches and fems (Kennedy and Davis 1993).

The struggles of Blacks provided gays and lesbians with new rhetoric and tactics. Just as the Black power movement declared that "Black is beautiful," for example, the gay rights movement asserted that "gay is good." Having witnessed sit-ins that forced the racial desegregation of lunch counters in the South, the Mattachine Society of New York sponsored a "sip-in" at a bar to protest police harassment of gay people (Adam 1995:77–78). In 1969, when the police raided a gay bar called the Stonewall in New York City's Greenwich Village, its patrons fought back. The ensuing riot burned down the bar and attracted a crowd of 2,000 people who battled with some 400 police officers amid cries of "Gay Power!" (D'Emilio 1983:232).

After the Stonewall rebellion, a gay liberation movement grew rapidly, spreading within two years to cities and campuses across North America, Western Europe, and Australia (Adam 1995:89). During its most radical phase, from 1969 to 1972, the gay liberation movement was closely linked to the New Left, spawning organizations such as the Gay Liberation Front and attracting participants who saw themselves as revolutionaries (Adam 1995:82; Licata 1981:178–81). However, more conventional reform groups were also organizing at the same time, many of them within established institutions such as churches (Adam 1995:89). When militant gay liberation groups, like other New Left groups, declined in the early seventies, the larger gay and lesbian rights movement continued.

Since the mid-1970s, the gay and lesbian movement has consisted of a diverse collection of organizations and activities in many countries (Adam 1995). Gay Pride Day parades are held annually in many cities, featuring drag queens and other flamboyant participants as well as more conventional members of gay communities. Lesbian feminists have developed extensive cultural activities and organizations, such as women's music festivals, book stores, presses, and journals. Gay civil rights organizations have formed to lobby governments for protections such as the inclusion of "sexual orientation" in human rights legislation and benefits such as health insurance and child custody rights associated with "domestic partnerships." Within established institutions such as churches, gay and lesbian members have formed caucuses to push for reforms such as gay marriage.

In the 1980s, after the Acquired Immune Deficiency Syndrome (AIDS) was identified as a disease that was killing many gay men, numerous new national and local organizations formed to serve the needs of AIDS victims and to pressure governments to deal with the crisis. Some of these new organizations were conventionally organized lobbying groups that "developed unprecedented, routinized connections to state institutions, welfare systems, and health bureaucracies" (Adam 1995:156). More radical groups, especially ACT UP (the AIDS Coalition to Unleash Power), engaged in confrontational tactics such as disruptive demonstrations (see Epstein 1996; Gamson 1989).

Moving beyond the AIDS issue in the 1990s, spin-off groups such as Queer Nation continued the use of the direct-action tactics pioneered by ACT UP. For example, activists occupied straight bars on "Nights Out" to raise heterosexual awareness of their existence (Trebay 1990). Advocates of "queer politics" see many mainstream gay organizations as homogenizing gay people and converting them into "replicas of heterosexual banality." Thus these activists have sought "to value and retain the particularity and difference developed in gay and lesbian cultural forms" (Adam 1995:146).

Movement Challenges to Gender and Family

In both its radical and reformist manifestations, the gay and lesbian movement represents fundamental challenges to conventional family and gender relations, which are connected to broader transformations in family and gender in the twentieth century. Gay and lesbian sexuality is part of the wider practice of nonmarital, nonreproductive sexuality. The alternative gender roles that may be adopted by gay men and lesbians are part of a larger movement toward less restrictive gender roles for men and women. And the new kinds of family forms that gays and lesbians create with children from previous marriages, adopted children, or children conceived through artificial insemination are part of the "postmodern" era in which new types of stepfamilies, single-parent families, and other alternative forms coexist with the conventional nuclear family (Stacey 1990). Not surprisingly, many resist all these social changes and desire a return to "traditional" family values. However, gays and lesbians also debate among themselves many issues related to sexuality and the family.

Sexuality

In the late 1960s and early 1970s, gay liberationists challenged traditional sexual norms by arguing for freedom of sexual expression outside the constraints of heterosexual, monogamous families (Adam 1995:84). To combat sexual repression and the nuclear family, some gay liberationists advocated public expressions of affection and the sharing of sex partners (p. 90). Gay men who settled in the Castro neighborhood of San Francisco made sexual freedom part of their lives, enjoying a "sexual free-for-all" in the bars and bathhouses of the gay community (FitzGerald 1986:56). Although the gay male community in San Francisco was particularly large and visible, compared with gay communities in most other cities, the championing of sexual freedom was a common theme of gay male liberation. These positions were an outgrowth of the counterculture of the 1960s, with its sexual experimentation and challenges to traditional morality, and did not seem extreme in that context.

Women, like men, experimented with sexual freedom in the 1960s, but they also came to question the sexism of men, such as the occupants of Berkeley's People's Park who called for "Free Land, Free Dope, Free Women" (Faderman 1991:203). Many women who became feminists in the late 1960s turned to lesbianism as a way of avoiding male sexism (see Cassell 1977). Feminists touted lesbianism as a superior form of love (Faderman 1991:205). Unlike gay men in communities such as the Castro, however, lesbians tended to be very private in their sexuality, engaging in serially monogamous relationships and stressing emotional ties (FitzGerald 1986:56–57; Kennedy and Davis 1993). Nevertheless, lesbian sexuality challenged traditional norms not only because it was nonreproductive, but also because it made men superfluous to women's pleasure.

In the early 1980s, communities such as the Castro had to face the problem of AIDS, a disease associated with sexual behavior. There was much conflict over how to do so, involving issues such as the closing of the gay baths in San Francisco. But, ultimately, the AIDS crisis brought people together in the effort to fight the disease and its spread (see FitzGerald 1986). Among gay men, the AIDS epidemic generated much discussion of "safe sex." Some retreated to monogomous lifestyles, and others sought ways to preserve sexual freedom in the age of AIDS (see Bawer 1993:174–75).

Debates about sexuality continue within gay and lesbian communities. For example, lesbians and feminists disagree strongly among themselves about issues such as sadomasochism and pornography (see Faderman 1991, chapter 10; Phelan 1989). In light of the AIDS epidemic, some gay writers publicly condemn some types of gay male sexual behavior (e.g., Kirk and Madsen 1989). "Queer theory" challenges the very division between "homosexuals" and "heterosexuals" that created the basis for a gay and lesbian rights movement. Within the movement, bisexuals and transgendered people demand recognition, leading to further questioning of the homosexual-heterosexual divide. In short, gay, lesbian, bisexual, and transgendered people are debating the place of sexuality in public and private life and forcing a reconsideration of the heterosexual standard of "normal sexuality."

Gender Roles and Family Forms

Beyond the issue of sexual practices, the gay and lesbian movement has challenged traditional gender roles and family forms. Early gay liberationists sometimes used dramatic means of raising consciousness. In Great Britain, for example, members of the Gay Liberation Front parodied gender norms by mixing fashions such as beards and dresses (Adam 1995:90). Such tactics were typically short-lived, as most people had to be more conventional in their everyday lives. However, gay men and lesbians have embraced a wide range of personal styles that do not necessarily conform to conventional gender norms. Within gay and lesbian communities, men can be "feminine" and women can be "masculine" and still find acceptance.

Same-sex partnerships present a challenge to traditional ideas of marriage and the family. In many places, gay rights activists have fought for domestic partnership legislation to gain spousal benefits such as insurance coverage and bereavement leaves. In supporting such legislation in San Francisco in 1982, Harry Britt, a member of the Board of Supervisors, argued, "This legislation has one purpose in mind—to recognize that the relationships of gay people and straight people who are not married are as meaningful as those of people who marry" (quoted in Thomas 1986:38). As this comment suggests, it is not only the concrete benefits that are at stake in domestic partnership legislation but the legitimacy of same-sex relationships.

Some movement activists also support gay marriage, although there is much debate within gay communities over this issue. Andrew Sullivan (1996a), an advocate of gay marriage, argues:

> People ask us why we want the right to marry, but the answer is obvious. It's the same reason anyone wants the right to marry. At some point in our lives, some of us are lucky enough to meet the person we truly love. And we want to commit to that person in front of our family and country for the rest of our lives. It's the most simple, the most natural, the most human instinct in the world. How could anyone seek to oppose that?

Some gays and lesbians oppose this position, however, on the grounds that gay people should value their differences from straight people rather than trying to emulate them. Still others are themselves uncomfortable with gay marriage for more traditional reasons or because they fear that it will alienate potential supporters. For example, the gay bartender of a Canton, Ohio, bar who was interviewed by the *New York Times* in a story on gays in "middle America" said of gay marriage: "I don't like it. I'm a devout Catholic. I don't believe two men should go before God to be joined in holy matrimony." A gay patron of the bar said he understood why President Clinton had signed the Republican-sponsored Defense of Marriage Act, which bans federal recognition of same-sex marriages. "The words 'gay marriage' scare straight people to death," he said (*New York Times*, September 22, 1996).

Regardless of whether gays and lesbians are allowed to legally marry, they are living together and often having children in new kinds of families. Just as second marriages often result in complex stepfamilies, gay and lesbian families may be complicated departures from the conventional nuclear family. For example, a Canadian baby was recently born to a lesbian couple and a gay male couple who are all good friends. The biological mother is Candace, the lesbian partner of Diana. The father is Patrick, the gay partner of Douglas. Because they felt it was unfair that they did not qualify for benefits available to heterosexual couples at the company where Patrick and Candace both work, Candace married Douglas and Patrick married Diana. The couples live near each other and are all involved in parenting the new baby, receiving help from friends and some members of their extended families (*Globe and Mail*, October 5, 1996). Although this arrangement was unusual enough to be profiled in a national newspaper, numerous gay and lesbian couples are having children through such means as adoption, artificial insemination, and arrangements between lesbians and gay men or other male friends and relatives.

Gay and lesbian families may serve as prototypes of nonnuclear families, in which people other than the biological or adoptive parents are involved in the raising of children. Members of a larger gay and lesbian community sometimes help couples in meeting the needs of their children. For example, support groups for gay and lesbian parents have sprung up in many cities. The involvement of a larger community of people in parenting is a departure from the idea that children are the concern and responsibility of their parents alone.

Although lesbian and gay parents face many of the problems common to all parents, same-sex parents also face special problems, some of which may be similar to those faced by stepparents. How, for example, is the role of the second parent to be defined? When his teacher asked who his father's partner was, a six-year-old boy replied, "That's my Dad's husband"; the two men had, in fact, been united by a minister (*Newsweek*, March 12, 1990). Gay and lesbian families require social recognition of new categories of relationships that are not easy even to name. As a lesbian couple raising a daughter conceived by one of them through artificial insemination noted, this is difficult even within gay and lesbian communities.

> Banned in several states in the United States, *Heather Has Two Mommies* is a children's book by Leslea Newman that depicts a lesbian family with, as the title suggests, two mothers. It reflects an orthodoxy in the way gay people are supposed to parent, at least according to certain paradigms established within the gay and lesbian community. It underscores the fact that even gay-positive literature reinforces the ingrained notion of "mommy" and "daddy," leaving unchallenged the assumption that a parent must be either one or the other. (Bernstein and Stephenson 1995)

Same-sex parents, like stepparents, represent a departure from the idea that "normal" families consist of biological or adoptive mothers and fathers and their children.

Countermovement Reactions

In response to gay and lesbian movements, countermovements have arisen that denounce homosexuality as a threat to "traditional family values." Since the 1970s, anti-gay groups in North America have worked to overturn gay rights measures and to pass legislation designed to discriminate against gay men and lesbians. Their hostility stems from concerns about social change related to gender and family.

The Gay Rights Controversy

Since the late seventies, conservatives in the United States have organized numerous campaigns to limit society's acceptance of same-sex sexuality. The first major effort occurred in Dade County, Florida, where a group called Save Our Children led a successful campaign to repeal a six-month-old ordinance that prohibited discrimination on the grounds of "sexual orientation." The leader of Save Our Children, evangelical performer Anita Bryant, then embarked on a speaking tour across the United States and Canada. As part of this crusade, a gay rights law was defeated by referendum in St. Paul, Minnesota, in April 1978; gay rights laws were repealed in Wichita, Kansas, and Eugene, Oregon, in May of the same year; and the Oklahoma state legislature passed a law allowing the dismissal of teachers who "advocate" or "practice" homosexuality (Adam 1995:111). In Arkansas, the state legislature passed a similar law banning homosexual teachers from the public schools and also denied credentials to homosexual pediatricians and social workers (FitzGerald 1986:67).

In 1978, conservative Californians attempted to pass a referendum known as the Briggs initiative, which would have allowed the dismissal of teachers who were involved in "encouraging, or promoting private or public homosexual activity . . . likely to come to the attention of children" (quoted in Adam 1995:112). The initiative's sponsor, State Senator John Briggs, circulated pamphlets associating homosexuality with child molestation and pornography (FitzGerald 1986:67). In response to the threat, some 30 organizations formed to oppose the Briggs initiative (Adam 1995:112), and San Francisco Supervisor Harvey Milk (who was later assassinated) engaged in a series of debates against John Briggs. Joined by unions, gay rights groups were successful in defeating the Briggs initiative. At the same time in Seattle, voters decided to retain a gay rights law, and the anti-gay campaign lost momentum (Adam 1995:113).

Efforts to defeat gay rights ordinances and to pass discriminatory legislation continue. In 1992, for example, voters in Colorado approved a referendum banning civil rights protections for gays and lesbians, but the law was overturned by the U.S. Supreme Court in 1996. Numerous anti–gay rights campaigns have taken place in other U.S. cities as well, leading *Newsweek* to report "a well-coordinated counteroffensive by the religious right" intended to stop "what its leaders regard as an intolerable gay advance out of the closet and into the social mainstream" (*Newsweek*, September 14, 1992). Even in Canada, where most provinces now prohibit discrimination on the basis of "sexual orientation" in their Human Rights Codes, there was a major battle over gay rights in Ontario in 1986. A coalition led by New Christian Right activists attempted to block the province from amending its Human Rights Code to include sexual orientation (see Herman 1994).

Reasons for Hostility

To explain the hostility that is often provoked by gay and lesbian rights movements, we need to examine the concerns of the countermovement in the context of social changes in gender and family. For many of its opponents, homosexuality symbolizes the changes that have occurred in parental relations with children, gender roles, sexual behavior, and family form. Gay and lesbian partnerships are yet another variety of lifestyle in an era characterized by frequent divorce, stepfamilies, single-parent families, and other departures from the intact nuclear family. Homosexuality, like premarital and extramarital sex, is part of a trend toward nonreproductive sexuality. Gay and lesbian relationships necessarily redefine gender roles and are part of a broader questioning of traditional "masculinity" and "femininity." The ability of young people to declare their homosexuality against their parents' wishes (however painful this step may be) is part of a more general trend toward independence among youth.

A concern with children is prominent in anti-gay efforts, such as Anita Bryant's "Save Our Children" campaign and attempts to ban homosexual teachers from the schools. Anti-gay activists worry that homosexuals will recruit children to become homosexuals. For example, Anita

Bryant's campaign used the slogan "Homosexuals cannot reproduce, so they must recruit," and she argued that the Dade County ordinance banning discrimination against homosexuals would allow "militant homosexuals" to "influence children to their abnormal way of life" (Miller 1995:402). Opponents of gay rights also fear that the children of lesbian and gay couples will become homosexuals.

Some believe that gay men are likely to be child molesters. In debating Harvey Milk over the Briggs initiative, John Briggs claimed:

> Pornographers want your children. Dope addicts want your children. Homosexuals want your children. They don't have any children of their own. If they don't recruit children or very young people, they'd all die away. They have no means of replenishing. That's why they want to be teachers and be equal status and have those people serve as role models and encourage people to join them. (Quoted in Shilts 1982:230)

Harvey Milk countered that "children do need protection—protection from the incest and child beatings pandemic in the heterosexual family." He asked, "How do you teach homosexuality—like French?" (Shilts 1982:230–31) and noted that most gays and lesbians are raised by heterosexual parents. Milk countered the claim that gay men are child molesters by arguing that heterosexual men are more likely to sexually abuse children. Despite such refutations, however, the fears remain, perhaps because the threat of "recruitment" by homosexuals symbolizes parents' fears about a general loss of control over their children.

Fundamentalist Christians, in particular, feel that their values are under siege and that they are losing their children to the secular culture (Herman 1994; Oberschall 1993). These fears are stoked by political organizations such as the Christian Voice, which sent the following message in a fundraising letter:

> Dear Friend:
>   I am rushing you this urgent letter because the children in your neighborhood are in danger.
>   How would you feel if tomorrow your child . . .
>   . . . was taught by a practicing homosexual?
>   . . . was bused 20 to 30 miles away to school every morning?
>   . . . was forced to attend classes in a school where all religion is banned?
>   If you think this could never happen . . . you are in for a shock!
> (Quoted in Crawford 1980:146)

Insofar as schools and governments do promote such values as tolerance of diversity and separation of church and state, which are at odds with the beliefs of some parents, the fears expressed by these fundamentalist

Christians are not unrealistic. Gays and lesbians become the symbolic scapegoats for parental fears, however, and false ideas persist, such as the belief that gay men are likely to be child molesters.

Concern about children is related to a larger concern about the "traditional" family. For fundamentalist Christians, marriage is a sacred institution, and "lifelong, legally sanctioned, heterosexual unions" are the basis of family life (Herman 1994:84). Nor is the view of "the family" as a cherished institution threatened by homosexuals limited to fundamentalist Christians. Conservative Canadian columnist Barbara Amiel, for example, has also commented on the importance of marriage as a social institution and the threat posed by proposals to recognize same-sex unions or to allow gays and lesbians to marry (Amiel 1994, 1996). In Amiel's view, marriage is a special institution "designed for the raising of families and the biological continuation of our species" (1994). Because homosexual unions do not produce children, they violate the specific purpose of marriage and cannot be considered legitimate. Amiel argues that marriage and the family have already been devastated by such trends as no-fault divorce laws, stigma-free illegitimacy, and state interference in child rearing; social recognition of same-sex marriages "will be the final acknowledgement of the social meaninglessness of the union between man and woman that was marriage" (1996).

Same-sex relationships are also associated with the erosion of traditional gender roles. For some women, homosexuality, like the Equal Rights Amendment and legal abortion, threatens their ability to keep a family together and create a happy home. As Anita Bryant complained during her anti–gay rights campaign, "so many married men with children who don't have a happy marriage are going into the homosexual bars for satisfaction" (quoted in Adam 1995:117). For women who find their identity in the role of homemaker, the availability of homosexual relationships competes with the feminine attractions of wives and homes.

For men who gain their sense of manhood from their heterosexuality, homosexuality represents a threat to masculinity. This threat was illustrated dramatically in the 1995 "Jenny Jones murder." In this instance, a man who spoke of his attraction to another man on the Jenny Jones talk show was murdered three days later by the man who was the object of his attention. Historian Jonathan Katz commented, "There's a fragility of masculinity that's challenged when a heterosexual man suddenly becomes an object. . . . You might say this murder is a way of more aggressively coming out as a heterosexual by someone who feels challenged" (*New York Times*, March 19, 1995).

Opposition to same-sex sexuality is also fueled by concerns about changing sexual mores. Traditionalists oppose homosexuality on the grounds that it is nonprocreative sex. The discourse of the New Christian Right also emphasizes the depravity of male homosexuality (Herman 1994:90). When the AIDS epidemic hit, some fundamentalists declared the disease a punishment from God. Interestingly, condemnations of homosexuality typically refer exclusively to gay men; "lesbians are notably absent from the discussion" (Herman 1994:86). This imbalance may have to do with the particular threat of gay male sexuality to the dominant conception of masculinity and to the challenges posed by gay activists who champion sexual liberation.

In San Francisco in the 1970s, Dianne Feinstein, then president of the city's Board of Supervisors, warned the gay male community about a potential backlash against publicly visible sex and against fads such as the wearing of spiked collars and other attire associated with sadomasochism. In an interview published in a gay newspaper, she expressed her support for gay people but said, "What I see happening in San Francisco—in the bar scene, in the street scene, in the S and M scene—is an imposition of lifestyle on those who do not wish to participate in that lifestyle" (quoted in FitzGerald 1986:65). Of course, gay sexuality was not particularly visible to people who lived outside areas such as the Castro district, but opponents of gay rights have used images of promiscuity among gay men in their arguments against the "normality" of homosexuality.

Some advocates of gay and lesbian rights argue that they should cultivate a vision of sexual liberation and acceptance of difference, despite threats of backlash; gay people are creating unique and positive communities that should be encouraged. Others argue that the public image of gays and lesbians is distorted. Bruce Bawer (1993) notes that there are all kinds of gay people with all types of lifestyles but that the "gay subculture" tends to emphasize the sexual aspect of homosexuality. Much of the annual Gay Pride Day march in New York, he argues, is "silly, sleazy, and sex-centered" (Bawer 1993:154) rather than representative of all gays and lesbians. At the same time, Bawer recognizes that gay men and lesbians are often shut out of the conventional world of heterosexual marriage. He describes the painful experience that he and his partner had participating in the wedding party of good friends and hearing it declared in the marriage ceremony that marriage between a man and a woman is "the only valid foundation for an enduring home" (p. 261). The experience reinforced Bawer's conviction that gay unions need to be legally recognized, either as marriages or domestic partnerships, so that gay men and lesbians can live in recognized families just like everyone else.

Conclusion

The battle over gay and lesbian rights, like the conflicts over the Equal Rights Amendment and abortion, must be understood in the context of large-scale social changes affecting family and gender. Different social groups have felt threatened by gays and lesbians at different times in part because homosexuality symbolizes broader concerns. In the early twentieth century, middle-class men felt their sense of manhood threatened by bureaucratic workplaces, working-class men and immigrants, and women entering the public sphere. It was middle-class men, rather than working-class men, who first felt the need to distance themselves from "fairies" and declare their manhood through exclusive heterosexuality. During the Depression, when many men lost their ability to prove their manhood as breadwinners, homosexuality seemed more threatening than ever.

The gay and lesbian rights movement arose in the context of changing gender and family relations, and the movement continues to promote such changes as flexible gender roles, new family forms, and sexual freedom. Some conservative groups, such as fundamentalist Christians, are particularly worried that their values and lifestyles are endangered. Consequently, a strong countermovement has mobilized in response to the gay and lesbian rights movement.

There is also much public debate, and debate within gay communities, over the issues raised by the movement. Some people applaud the gay and lesbian movement for generating new models of community, including welcome experiments with new family forms that provide relief to individual parents struggling in isolation with the demands of child rearing. To others, the proliferation of new family forms and the expansion of outside influences on children are a threat to the already beleaguered nuclear family and the rights of parents to control their own children. Among gay people, the movement subculture is viewed by some as a model of tolerance for diversity and sexual freedom and by others as an impediment to their efforts to fit into mainstream society and to be themselves without appearing threatening.

NOTE

1. The term *gay* was used as a code word in the context of homosexual activites, and became "the preeminent term (for gay men among gay men)" with the establishment of a split between "homosexuals" and "heterosexuals" by the 1940s (Chauncey 1994:14). Donald Webster Cory (1951) says that the term

probably originated with the French in the sixteenth century and notes its usefulness as a code word for women as well as men, although it was used more frequently by men.

7

The Contribution
of Social Movements

We have seen widespread changes over the past couple of centuries in the lives of all women and men. Because of fundamental socioeconomic changes, women now have a great deal of freedom to pursue education and careers. Men are less confined to the breadwinning role and better able to participate in family life as well as public life.

Social movements, including women's movements and a range of other movements, have played an important role in promoting such changes in response to the opportunities created by large-scale transformations. For example, women's movements have been able to push for job opportunities for women after economic shifts produced more jobs in the service sector of the economy.

Nevertheless, important obstacles to new gender and family relations remain. Many of these barriers are related to the structures of jobs and the economy as well as prevailing gender ideologies. Because of race and class stratification, there are still significant differences among women in opportunities for education and careers. Men who want to care for their children and act as equal partners in the home are confronted with strong obstacles such as the need to work long hours at their jobs (Gerson 1993). Women who work outside the home still tend to shoulder much of the household work as well (Hochschild 1989). Both men and women face a work world that is not geared to family life, and parents typically receive little social support in raising children.

Change is also difficult because movements that seek to transform gender and family relations often provoke strong countermovements. Movement goals, such as the Equal Rights Amendment and laws establishing equal rights for gays and lesbians, often appear to threaten the values and lifestyles of others. Indeed, movements frequently aim to challenge the dominant culture, introducing new ways of thinking and living. It may not be possible, then, for movements to change the culture without creating a backlash.

This concluding chapter will review some of the efforts of social movements to promote social changes in gender relations, including the circumstances under which some movements have succeeded without provoking substantial opposition. It will also look at the types of concerns expressed by opponents of gender-change movements. The goal is to understand the sorts of issues that movement activists need to address and the common ground that movements and their opponents may share. Finally, the chapter will note some of the limits to changes in gender and family relations that social movements can produce.

Movements and Countermovements

Arguably, social movements have succeeded in many ways in promoting social changes related to gender and family, even in the face of opposition to those changes. For example, the abortion rights movement succeeded in making legal abortion widely available, even though legalization of abortion provoked a strong countermovement. New ideas such as same-sex marriage have become the subject of public discourse, despite much opposition to such proposals. Bringing new practices and ideas into the realm of discourse and possibility is a significant achievement. Nevertheless, movements would surely prefer to avoid backlash if possible.

In some instances, movements have successfully altered gender and family relations without creating countermovements. Several historical examples suggest that movements can accomplish this feat by building on existing understandings rather than directly challenging dominant cultural ideas. Of course, significant movements need to change the existing culture, but they may produce this result indirectly. The temperance movement, for example, did not appear to threaten existing cultural values but ultimately contributed to the expansion of women's roles (Giele 1995). The movement built on existing understandings by using maternalist rhetoric and adopting the rituals of evangelical religion at its meetings. Yet the movement extended women's role out of the home and offered a new vision of community in which people took responsibility for the welfare of others.

Women's Strike for Peace, similarly, used maternalist language and did not intentionally challenge conventional gender roles. The group was even able to attract the support of Phyllis Schlafly, who would later lead the opposition to the Equal Rights Amendment (Swerdlow 1993:94). Women's Strike for Peace succeeded by expanding the role of mother, emphasizing women's concern for the world rather than for their own families only. The organization did not threaten existing gender ideologies, but it ultimately helped to build feminist consciousness.

Another example of creating change without stirring up backlash is provided by women's self-help movements, such as the postpartum depression (PPD) and breast cancer self-help movements (Taylor 1996; Taylor and Van Willigen 1996). Women's self-help movements also make frequent use of maternalist language, and they reach a constituency of women who would otherwise not come into contact with the women's movement. Yet the self-help movements have also challenged societal views of appropriate feminine behavior. For example, the PPD support movement has challenged the idea that women automatically love their children by revealing the struggles of women fighting depression at the births of their children. The breast cancer support movement has disputed the idea that losing a breast makes a woman somehow less feminine and is something that should be hidden. Women's self-help movements also promote new forms of community, including support groups and phone, e-mail, and pen-pal networks, bringing women out of their families and into a wider community of support.

In all of these examples, the movements did not set out to challenge existing gender roles or family relations. They attracted large numbers of women who would not necessarily call themselves feminists. But the movements enlarged women's roles and helped to build community networks outside of nuclear family life. In the temperance movement, middle-class women took up the problems of working-class women and tried to make cities more livable. Women's Strike for Peace activists extended their caring to the children and women of the world who were suffering from war. Women's self-help movements have created communities of support based on the ethics of caring and emotion. In short, a positive vision of community has made these movements highly attractive to feminists and nonfeminists alike.

Movements that have generated controversy have been less successful in promoting a positive vision of collective concern, and they have also appeared threatening to the values of some groups. In the case of the Equal Rights Amendment, there was strong public support for the abstract values of equality and individual rights. But to those who felt threatened by the ERA, it seemed that the women's movement was promoting the individual rights of women at the expense of the things they valued in female culture. The ERA seemed to threaten the value of sacrifice for one's family and the positive role of the homemaker in creating a nurturing environment apart from the competitive male world. It seemed to free men to abdicate their family responsibilities. The ERA, along with rising divorce rates, symbolized some women's fears that their world was in jeopardy. The pro-ERA movement did not succeed in replacing their fears with a vision of a world in which both men and women would take equal responsibility for home and family.

In the case of the abortion conflict, the pro-choice movement did build on existing culture to some extent. By the time reformers began to advocate legalization of abortion in the 1960s, family planning had gained widespread acceptance. The idea of planning families is a very mainstream, middle-class notion. A majority of Americans believe that abortion should be legal, at least in some situations. They do not, for example, believe that a family should necessarily allow a child with severe defects to be born (see Cook et al. 1992).

Feminists, however, have not adhered to the middling pro-choice position favored by a majority of the public, and this has helped to provoke opposition. Moreover, many who oppose abortion have religious objections that will not be met by any version of the pro-choice position, conservative or radical. However, opposition to abortion is also fueled by some of the same concerns as opposition to the ERA. Abortion is seen as a selfish choice, made by women who are pursuing individual rather than collective interests and forsaking the nurturant role of wife and mother.

In reality, feminists have always been concerned about collective responsibilities as well as individual rights. In some public campaigns, however, the individual rights approach has overshadowed the collective approach—in part because our political culture is geared toward individual rights (Morton 1992; Bortner 1990) and in part because a "rights" approach has broad appeal. For example, the idea that a woman has a right to control her own body has diffused widely and helps attract young women to the abortion rights movement.

Moreover, it is difficult for a movement to enlarge its focus when a countermovement is waging a single-issue campaign. In the 1970s, for example, some feminists tried to broaden the abortion debate to talk about jobs, child care, and all of the social supports necessary to allow women to make positive choices about having children. At a time when the anti-abortion movement was threatening the very legality of abortion, however, the pro-choice movement could hardly afford to fight for multiple issues (see Staggenborg 1991). Ultimately, though, feminists must address these larger concerns if they are to achieve meaningful change in gender and family relations.

Work, Family, and Community

As anyone who has raised children and tried to run a household knows, it's a lot of work. The amount of energy required for home maintenance tasks such as cleaning, laundry, grocery shopping, and meal preparation is enormous. Add children, and homemaking is easily a full-time job. One problem is that the value of this work has never been fully recognized. Among women who have devoted themselves to the housewife role, this lack of recognition may cause resentment at a feminist movement that seems to be further devaluing the homemaker. For men who might be inclined to choose full-time homemaking, the lack of social value placed on this choice is a powerful disincentive (Gerson 1993).

Another problem is that in many households, both mothers and fathers need to work outside the home, leaving little time for family life. Between 1960 and 1992, women's rate of participation in the U.S. labor force rose from 38 to 58 percent (Costello and Stone 1994:281). Today, over half of mothers with children under one year old work outside the home. To remain in the middle class, most families now require two wage earners. For single-parent families, full-time homemaking is rarely an option, particularly with changes in welfare laws requiring public-aid recipients to find employment. And beyond the issue of financial need, many men and women want jobs outside the home because they find fulfillment in work. At the same time, many also want to have children and a family life. The problem is how to have both.

Regardless of the demands of outside work, parents need support in raising children. They require help in knowing what to do in various situations, they need some time to themselves away from children, and they need to share the burdens and joys of parenting with other people who care about their children. Extended family members are traditional sources of advice, babysitting, financial help, and other support. In a mobile society, however, many couples and single parents do not live in the same cities as their own parents or siblings. Others may not wish to depend heavily on their extended families for various reasons. Frequently, family members are themselves busy with jobs and such obligations as care of elderly parents. Given these realities, parents typically need community support, but it is not always available.

What do social movements offer toward resolution of these problems? Critics of gender-change movements such as the women's movement often feel that they promote individualism at the expense of collective responsibility. These critics see feminists, for example, as pursuing their own careers and devaluing sacrifice for the good of the family. In fact, however, many social movements have promoted collective concerns along with individual fulfillment and have created new forms of community (see Lichterman 1996). Although they have sometimes excluded outsiders, movements have developed new models of community responsibility, which have the potential of appealing to many people. But often movement communities are invisible to those outside their boundaries.

In the New Left of the 1960s, activists were engaged in "prefigurative politics" (Breines 1989). That is, they were working to create a movement that would reflect the kind of society they wanted. Movement activists therefore attempted to develop collective forms of decision making and to involve everyone in the process. Although these efforts were not always successful, participants often experienced what seemed like an ideal form of community. For example, participants in the Free University founded at Berkeley described how "graduate students taught in the stairwells. . . . We set up a kitchen and a first aid station. Blankets were distributed. We governed ourselves. Peace and order prevailed" (quoted in Breines 1989:32). Even some nondemocratic aspects of the movement, such as sexism, produced efforts at correction. Most notably, a women's movement devoted to developing a better version of participatory democracy emerged from the New Left.

Within the women's movement, there have been many efforts to create caring communities. Before abortion was legalized, feminists often formed referral networks to help women get safe abortions. For example, in Chicago a collective of women known as "Jane" eventually became involved in providing abortions to women. In doing so, they created a caring atmosphere that was in stark contrast to the conditions faced by many women seeking illegal abortions (Kaplan 1995). Similarly, feminists have created many rape crisis services that provide understanding help to rape victims. Feminists active in rape crisis work often help train police officers, hospital workers, and other service workers in how to deal with rape victims, thereby creating a more humane community of support for women. Lesbian feminists have created various institutions apart from the mainstream culture that are based on a belief in "female values" such as egalitarianism, collectivism, caring, and cooperation (Taylor and Rupp 1993).

All kinds of feminist groups have typically provided services such as child care for their members. The National Women's Music Festival, a four-day event dominated by lesbian feminists, provides child care, community housing, and signing for the deaf at concerts in its attempt to create a prefigurative community once a year (Eder, Staggenborg, and

Sudderth 1995; Staggenborg, Eder, and Sudderth 1993–94). The festival tries to create an atmosphere in which everyone is accepted and concerns with matters such as how women look are set aside. One participant described her reaction the first time she attended the festival:

> The atmosphere was so female. I wear mascara—I'm the kind of person who feels she can't go out without mascara! But there I didn't feel I had to worry about how I looked. I felt freer—that's the word I've been looking for to describe the experience—it was a feeling of freedom. (Quoted in Eder et al. 1995:493)

Another participant, who attended the festival in a wheelchair, described her experience of the festival community:

> [S]omeone was always there to meet my car with a wheelchair. Everything I wanted to do was accessible. There was a sense of camaraderie with the other differently-abled people. I felt special—there wasn't any sense of having a stigma. I felt cared for. (Quoted in Eder et al. 1995:494)

Other movements have also created prefigurative communities. For example, the anti–nuclear power movement of the late 1970s was structured around "affinity groups" consisting of up to about 15 individuals who relied on one another to get them through experiences such as arrest (Epstein 1991:66). AIDS activists have created extensive services for people with the disease and a strong culture of support has developed in gay communities as a result (see Sullivan 1996b:62). In the environmental movement, local organizations have worked on creating communities that involve people in decision making and that sustain the activism of individuals for many years (Lichterman 1996).

Some of these efforts are directly related to the needs of families for support. When day care is provided at meetings and children are included in events, families with children can be integrated into a movement community. Some gay and lesbian communities provide models of alternatives to extended families. For example, support groups for gay and lesbian parents help make the concerns of families collective. In some instances, gay men and lesbians might share responsibility for parenting, thereby enlarging the circle of people who care intensely about a child. More commonly, same-sex parents often make a special effort to ensure that their children relate to members of the opposite sex (Kantrowitz 1996:57). In some cases, this effort relies on extended family members, but in other cases it relies on friends who are brought into the family.

Ironically, extended gay and lesbian families are not always so different from divorce-extended families in evangelical Christian communities.

Judith Stacey (1990), in *Brave New Families*, describes Pam and Al, a Christian couple who formed a close relationship with Pam's ex-husband, Don, and his cohabiting partner, Shirley. The two couples lived next door to each other, socialized together, and were all involved with the children from Pam and Don's marriage. One of the daughters, Katie, became part of a communal Christian evangelical group after her marriage. After the birth of her first child, Katie and another woman in the community cared for their children cooperatively and shared housework. The members of several households in the community were in constant contact with one another through Bible study groups, dinners together, and their work running food and clothing banks and other missionary activities (Stacey 1990:100–101).

Although communal living arrangements do not appeal to everyone, many social movements offer models of collective support for families and expanded gender roles. These efforts to create community life are attractive to many people, conservatives and liberals alike. For example, young women who embrace feminism are attracted by the community they find with like-minded women (Goldner and Dill 1995). Of course, groups want communities that promote their values. Evangelical Christians and lesbian feminists are looking for different things. Nevertheless, they have some shared concerns. Some feminist values have even influenced conservative Christians. For example, an evangelical minister described the problems with marriage: "One of the greatest failures in marriage is communication. The husband is afraid to reveal his emotions. Women are generally much better at this. A man needs to learn to open up emotionally, to cry on his wife's shoulders" (quoted in Stacey 1990:120).

The Challenge of Gender

Support for changing gender relations within families can come from diverse sources. However, evangelical ministers typically believe in separate spheres for men and women, and feminists would typically like to promote equal sharing between husbands and wives with regard to work and family roles. Many antifeminist women do not believe such sharing is possible or desirable. They see feminism as freeing men from their breadwinning responsibilities rather than bringing them into partnership with women. They see women carrying a double burden of home and work rather than being liberated by the opportunity to pursue careers.

In fact, women who work outside the home do frequently perform a disproportionate share of the housework as well. The National Survey of Families and Households, conducted in the United States in 1987–88, shows that women employed outside the home report doing an average of 33.2 hours of housework per week, while employed men report doing 18.2 hours per week (Lennon and Rosenfield 1994:517). However, this outcome may have less to do with gender role socialization than with the enormous obstacles that stand in the way of equal partnerships (Gerson 1993).

Many men who would like to become more involved husbands and fathers cannot do so—not because they are addicted to their jobs but because of the financial needs of the family. Because women's jobs typically pay less than men's jobs, few men can afford to quit work while their wives support the family or to work part-time so that they can spend more time at home. In addition, society tends to disapprove of men who choose not to pursue careers (Gerson 1993:245). And even if the financial and social obstacles could be overcome, part-time jobs are rarely available to men, particularly in male-dominated fields. As a male sanitation worker commented:

> If it was feasible, I would love to spend more time with my child. That would be more important to me than working. I'd love to be able to work twenty-five hours a week or four days a week and have three days off to spend with the family, but most jobs aren't going to accommodate you that way. (Quoted in Gerson 1993:247)

Men and women who want both meaningful work and time with their families face a basic problem: The world of work remains gendered. Although families have been changing dramatically, the structure of most jobs still assumes that a full-time homemaker is available to take care of family needs. Consequently, jobs are not organized to allow people time at home, and the problems of families are considered private ones, to be handled by people on their own. Yet men and women are forced to make decisions about family life, such as when they will have children and how they will care for them, based on the rhythms of work.

Most professions have a "clockwork" based on a male career model (Hochschild 1994). Women who wish to succeed in many careers must postpone childbearing, often until their late thirties. A woman who pursues an academic career, for example, might spend much of her twenties in graduate school. After beginning a tenure-track job, she must devote a great deal of time to publishing to achieve tenure. If she chooses to have children in her twenties or early thirties, she may well fail to keep her job in a system that requires a large volume of production early in the career.

Similarly, in a corporate career it is very difficult to have children before being promoted to the higher ranks of a firm (Hertz 1986:206). As one woman explained:

> All of us know that having a child could mean the difference between getting a promotion and not getting a promotion. . . . You can't gain time getting something in the year in which you have a child. I mean, that may be the only year for three years that something might come up that would mean you could get a promotion. (Quoted in Hertz 1986:125)

Once people in demanding careers have children, heavy workloads and frequent travel make it hard to spend sufficient time with them.

Social movements can address some, but not all, of these problems. For example, movements can pressure governments to enact measures such as the 1993 Family and Medical Leave Act (FMLA). It requires employers to give people time off for events such as the birth of a child or the illness of a family member. Although the leave is unpaid, the benefits and job of the employee are protected. However, the legislation applies only to firms of a certain size, so that no more than 60 percent of the workforce is covered (Vogel 1995:128). Despite its limitations, the FMLA is important in that it forces employers to recognize that workers have family needs (Vogel 1995:136). Significantly, the legislation allows men as well as women to take time off to care for their families.

Sometimes employers, particularly those who rely on large numbers of female employees, take the initiative in seeking solutions to problems such as child care that create absenteeism and turnover. For example, some employers are providing benefits such as on-site child-care centers (see Auerbach 1988). Often, however, the demands of workplaces encourage individual solutions. For example, corporate workers often employ their own full-time babysitters to give them the flexibility of working long hours (Hertz 1986). They rarely make collective demands on their employers because the culture of the corporate workplace encourages them to act as individuals, competing with fellow employees rather than joining together to solve common problems (Hertz 1986:18–19).

Conclusion

Further changes in gender and family relations can be expected as current trends, such as the entry of greater numbers of women into the labor force, continue. Social movements, too, will continue to advance new understandings of gender and family. But movements and countermovements will inevitably clash as the values of different groups come into conflict. Movements that build on existing understandings are likely to be most successful in changing culture without creating backlash. Those that offer a positive vision of community may be especially attractive to people of divergent ideological persuasions.

Social movements face enormous difficulties in trying to bring about collective solutions to the problems of families because they face individualistic political and corporate cultures and gendered institutions. Nevertheless, social movements are essential in expanding our consciousness about the possibilities open to men and women. Large-scale socioeconomic and political changes produce opportunities for new gender and family relations, but social movements introduce new ideas and ways of living into our lives.

References

Acker, Joan. 1990. "Hierarchies, Jobs, Bodies: A Theory of Gendered Organizations." *Gender and Society* 4(2):139–58.

Adam, Barry D. 1995. *The Rise of a Gay and Lesbian Movement.* Rev. ed. Boston: Twayne.

Amiel, Barbara. 1994. "Ontario and Gays: A New Frontier?" *Maclean's,* June 6, p. 9.

———. 1996. "Sterile Unions." *The Gazette* (Montreal), September 21, p. B5.

Arrington, T. S. and P. A. Kyle. 1978. "Equal Rights Amendment Activists in North Carolina." *Signs* 3(Spring): 660–80.

Auerbach, Judith D. 1988. *In the Business of Childcare: Employer Initiatives and Working Women.* New York: Praeger.

Bawer, Bruce. 1993. *A Place at the Table.* New York: Poseidon Press.

Bernard, Jessie. 1981. "The Good-Provider Role: Its Rise and Fall." *American Psychologist* 36(1):1–12.

Bernstein, Jane and Laura Stephenson. 1995. "Dykes, Donors and Dry Ice: Alternative Insemination." Pp. 3–15 in *Lesbian Parenting,* edited by Katherine Arnup. Charlottetown, Prince Edward Island, Canada: Gynergy Books.

Black, Naomi. 1989. *Social Feminism.* Ithaca, NY: Cornell University Press.

Blanchard, Dallas A. 1994. *The Anti-Abortion Movement and the Rise of the Religious Right: From Polite to Fiery Protest.* New York: Twayne.

Boles, Janet K. 1979. *The Politics of the Equal Rights Amendment: Conflict and the Decision Process.* New York: Longman.

Bordin, Ruth. 1981. *Woman and Temperance: The Quest for Power and Liberty, 1873–1900.* Philadelphia: Temple University Press.

Bortner, M. A. 1990. "Reproductive Rights: The Necessity and Inadequacy of the Reproductive Rights Discourse." *Social Justice* 17(3):99–110.

Boston Women's Health Book Collective. 1992. "When Yogurt Was Illegal." *Ms.,* July/August, pp. 38–39.

Brady, David W. and Kent L. Tedin. 1976. "Ladies in Pink: Religion and Political Ideology in the Anti-ERA Movement." *Social Science Quarterly* 56(4):564–75.

Breines, Wini. 1989. *Community and Organization in the New Left, 1962–1968.* New Brunswick, NJ: Rutgers University Press.

————. 1992. *Young, White, and Miserable: Growing Up Female in the Fifties.* Boston: Beacon Press.

Brown, Phil and Faith I. T. Ferguson. 1995. "'Making a Big Stink': Women's Work, Women's Relationships, and Toxic Waste Activism." *Gender and Society* 9(2):145–72.

Buechler, Steven M. 1986. *The Transformation of the Woman Suffrage Movement: The Case of Illinois, 1850–1920.* New Brunswick, NJ: Rutgers University Press.

————. 1990. *Women's Movements in the United States.* New Brunswick, NJ: Rutgers University Press.

Buschman, Joan K. and Silvo Lenart. 1996. "'I Am Not a Feminist, But . . .': College Women, Feminism, and Negative Experiences." *Political Psychology* 17(1):59–75.

Cable, Sherry. 1992. "Women's Social Movement Involvement: The Role of Structural Availability in Recruitment and Participation Processes." *The Sociological Quarterly* 33(1):35–50.

Cassell, Joan. 1977. *A Group Called Women.* New York: David McKay.

Cassidy, Keith. 1995. "The Right to Life Movement: Sources, Development, and Strategies." *Journal of Policy History* 7(1):128–59.

Chafe, William. 1991. *The Paradox of Change: American Women in the 20th Century.* New York: Oxford University Press.

Chafetz, Janet S. and Anthony G. Dworkin. 1986. *Female Revolt: The Rise of Women's Movements in World and Historical Perspective.* Totowa, NJ: Rowman & Littlefield.

Chauncey, George. 1994. *Gay New York.* New York: Basic Books.

Cohen, Lizabeth. 1993. "The Great Depression and World War II." Pp. 189–203 in *Encyclopedia of American Social History,* edited by Mary K. Cayton, Elliott J. Gorn, and Peter W. Williams. New York: Scribner.

Condit, Celeste Michelle. 1990. *Decoding Abortion Rhetoric: Communicating Social Change.* Urbana: University of Illinois Press.

Connell, Robert W. 1990. "A Whole New World: Remaking Masculinity in the Context of the Environmental Movement." *Gender and Society* 4(4):452–78.

————. 1995. *Masculinities.* Berkeley: University of California Press.

Cook, Elizabeth A., Ted G. Jelen, and Clyde Wilcox. 1992. *Between Two Absolutes: Public Opinion and the Politics of Abortion.* Boulder, CO: Westview Press.

Coontz, Stephanie. 1992. *The Way We Never Were.* New York: Basic Books.

Cory, Donald Webster. 1951. *The Homosexual in America.* New York: Greenberg.

Costello, Cynthia and Anne J. Stone, eds. 1994. *The American Woman, 1994–95.* New York: W. W. Norton.

Cott, Nancy. 1978. *The Bonds of Womanhood.* New Haven, CT: Yale University Press.

———. 1986. "Feminist Theory and Feminist Movements." Pp. 49–62 in *What is Feminism?* edited by Juliet Mitchell and Ann Oakley. New York: Pantheon Books.

———. 1987. *The Grounding of Modern Feminism.* New Haven, CT: Yale University Press.

Crawford, Alan. 1980. *Thunder on the Right.* New York: Pantheon.

Cuneo, Michael. 1989. *Catholics against the Church: Anti-Abortion Protest in Toronto, 1969–1985.* Toronto: University of Toronto Press.

Daniels, Mark R., Robert Darcy, and Joseph W. Westphal. 1982. "The ERA Won—At Least in the Opinion Polls." *PS* 15(4):578–84.

Datapedia of the United States, 1790–2000. 1994. Compiled by George Thomas Kurian. Lanham, MD: Bernan Press.

Davis, Flora. 1991. *Moving the Mountain: The Women's Movement since 1960.* New York: Simon & Schuster.

D'Emilio, John. 1983. *Sexual Politics, Sexual Communities: The Making of a Homosexual Minority in the United States, 1940–1970.* Chicago: University of Chicago Press.

———. 1993. "Capitalism and Gay Identity." Pp. 467–76 in *The Lesbian and Gay Studies Reader,* edited by Henry Abelove, Michele A. Barale, and David M. Halperin. New York: Routledge.

——— and Estelle B. Freedman. 1988. *Intimate Matters: A History of Sexuality in America.* New York: Harper & Row.

Dubois, Ellen. 1978. *Feminism and Suffrage.* Ithaca, NY: Cornell University Press.

Douglas, Susan J. 1994. *Where the Girls Are: Growing Up Female with the Mass Media.* New York: Times Books.

Eder, Donna, Suzanne Staggenborg, and Lori Sudderth. 1995. "The National Women's Music Festival: Collective Identity and Diversity in a Lesbian-Feminist Community." *Journal of Contemporary Ethnography* 23(4):485–515.

Ehrenreich, Barbara. 1983. *Hearts of Men: American Dreams and the Flight from Commitment.* New York: Anchor Press.

Epstein, Barbara L. 1981. *The Politics of Domesticity.* Middletown, CT: Wesleyan University Press.

———. 1991. *Political Protest and Cultural Revolution: Nonviolent Direct Action in the 1970s and 1980s.* Berkeley: University of California Press.

Epstein, Steven. 1996. *Impure Science: AIDS, Activism, and the Politics of Knowledge.* Berkeley: University of California Press.

Evans, Sara. 1979. *Personal Politics: The Roots of Women's Liberation in the Civil Rights Movement and the New Left.* New York: Vintage Books.

Faderman, Lillian. 1991. *Odd Girls and Twilight Lovers: A History of Lesbian Life in Twentieth-Century America.* New York: Penguin.

Faludi, Susan. 1991. *Backlash: The Undeclared War against American Women.* New York: Crown.

Ferree, Myra Marx and Beth B. Hess. 1994. *Controversy and Coalition.* Rev. ed. New York: Twayne.

FitzGerald, Frances. 1986. *Cities on a Hill.* New York: Simon & Schuster.

Flexner, Eleanor. 1959. *Century of Struggle: The Woman's Rights Movement in the United States.* New York: Atheneum.

Francome, Colin. 1984. *Abortion Freedom—A Worldwide Movement.* Winchester, MA: Allen and Unwin.

Freeman, Jo. 1975. *The Politics of Women's Liberation.* New York: Longman.

Fried, Marlene Gerber. 1994. "Reproductive Wrongs." *The Women's Review of Books* 11(10–11):6–7.

Friedan, Betty. 1963. *The Feminine Mystique.* New York: Dell.

———. 1981. *The Second Stage.* New York: Summit Books.

Furstenberg, Frank F. 1988. "Good Dads—Bad Dads: Two Faces of Fatherhood." Pp. 193–218 in *The Changing American Family and Public Policy,* edited by Andrew J. Cherlin. Washington, DC: Urban Institute.

Gamson, Joshua. 1989. "Silence, Death, and the Invisible Enemy: AIDS Activism and Social Movement 'Newness.'" *Social Problems* 36:351–67.

Gans, Herbert J. 1979. *Deciding What's News.* New York: Vintage Books.

Gerson, Kathleen. 1985. *Hard Choices: How Women Decide about Work, Career, and Motherhood.* Berkeley: University of California Press.

———. 1986–87. "Emerging Social Divisions among Women: Implications for Welfare State Politics." *Politics and Society* 15(2):213–21.

———. 1993. *No Man's Land: Men's Changing Commitments to Family and Work.* New York: Basic Books.

Giele, Janet Z. 1995. *Two Paths to Women's Equality: Temperance, Suffrage, and the Origins of Modern Feminism.* New York: Twayne.

Gilbert, James. 1986. *A Cycle of Outrage: America's Reaction to the Juvenile Delinquent in the 1950s.* New York: Oxford University Press.

Ginsburg, Faye D. 1989. *Contested Lives: The Abortion Debate in an American Community.* Berkeley: University of California Press.

Gitlin, Todd. 1980. *The Whole World Is Watching.* Berkeley: University of California Press.

Globe and Mail (Toronto). 1996. "Family Matters." October 5, pp. D1–D2.

Goldner, Melinda and Kim Dill. 1995. "Explaining Post-Feminism: A Continuum of Responses to the Contemporary Women's Movement." Paper presented at the annual meeting of the American Sociological Association, Washington, DC.

Gorn, Elliot J. 1986. *The Manly Art: Bare-Knuckle Prize Fighting in America.* Ithaca, NY: Cornell University Press.

Granberg, Donald. 1978. "Pro-Life or Reflection of Conservative Ideology? An Analysis of Opposition to Legalized Abortion." *Sociology and Social Research* 62(3):414–29.

———. 1981. "The Abortion Activists." *Family Planning Perspectives* 13(4):157–63.

——— and Donald Denney. 1982. "The Coathanger and the Rose." *Society* 19(4):39–46.

——— and Beth Wellman Granberg. 1980. "Abortion Attitudes, 1965–1980: Trends and Determinants." *Family Planning Perspectives* 12(5):250–61.

Gusfield, Joseph. 1955. "Social Structure and Moral Reform: A Study of the Women's Christian Temperance Union." *American Journal of Sociology* 61:221–32.

———. 1966. *Symbolic Crusade: Status Politics and the American Temperance Movement.* Urbana: University of Illinois Press.

Hacker, Andrew. 1979. "Of Two Minds about Abortion." *Harper's,* January, pp. 16–22.

Hareven, Tamara K. 1987. "Historical Analysis of the Family." Pp. 37–57 in *Handbook of Marriage and the Family,* edited by Marvin B. Sussman and Suzanne K. Steinmetz. New York: Plenum Press.

Herman, Didi. 1994. *Rights of Passage: Struggles for Lesbian and Gay Legal Equality.* Toronto: University of Toronto Press.

Hersh, Blanche. 1978. *The Slavery of Sex: Feminist-Abolitionists in America.* Urbana: University of Illinois Press.

Hertz, Rosanna. 1986. *More Equal than Others: Women and Men in Dual-Career Marriages.* Berkeley: University of California Press.

Hochschild, Arlie. 1983. *The Managed Heart: Commercialization of Human Feeling.* Berkeley: University of California Press.

——— with Anne Machung. 1989. *The Second Shift: Working Parents and the Revolution at Home.* New York: Viking.

———. 1994. "Inside the Clockwork of Male Careers." Pp. 125–39 in *Gender and the Academic Experience,* edited by Kathryn P. Meadow Orlans and Ruth A. Wallace. Lincoln: University of Nebraska Press.

Hole, Judith and Ellen Levine. 1971. *Rebirth of Feminism.* New York: Quadrangle.

Ireland, Patricia. 1992. "The State of NOW: A Presidential (and Personal) Report." *Ms.,* July/August, pp. 24–27.

Isenberg, Nancy G. 1993. "Women's Organizations." Pp. 1667–76 in *Encyclopedia of American Social History,* edited by Mary K. Cayton, Elliott J. Gorn, and Peter W. Williams. New York: Scribner.

Jenson, Jane. 1987. "Changing Discourse, Changing Agendas: Political Rights and Reproductive Policies in France." Pp. 64–88 in *The Women's Movements of the United States and Western Europe,* edited by Mary F. Katzenstein and Carol M. Mueller. Philadelphia: Temple University Press.

Joffe, Carole. 1986–87. "Abortion and Antifeminism." *Politics and Society* 15(2):207–12.

Kantrowitz, Barbara. 1996. "Gay Families Come Out." *Newsweek,* November 4, pp. 50–57.

Kaplan, Laura. 1995. *The Story of Jane.* New York: Pantheon Books.

Katz, Jonathan Ned. 1995. *The Invention of Heterosexuality.* New York: Plume.

Keene, Karlyn H. 1991. "'Feminism' Vs. Women's Rights." *The Public Perspective* 3(1):3–4.

Kennedy, Elizabeth Lapovsky and Madeline D. Davis. 1993. *Boots of Leather, Slippers of Gold: The History of a Lesbian Community.* New York: Penguin.

Kerber, Linda K. 1980. *Women of the Republic: Intellect and Ideology in Revolutionary America.* New York: W. W. Norton.

Kimmel, Michael S. 1989. "From Pedestals to Partners: Men's Responses to Feminism." Pp. 581–94 in *Women: A Feminist Perspective,* 4th ed., edited by Jo Freeman. Mountain View, CA: Mayfield.

———. 1996. *Manhood in America: A Cultural History.* New York: Free Press.

King, Mary. 1987. *Freedom Song: A Personal Story of the 1960s Civil Rights Movement.* New York: William Morrow.

Kirk, Marshall and Hunter Madsen. 1989. *After the Ball.* New York: Doubleday.

Klatch, Rebecca. 1987. *Women of the New Right.* Philadelphia: Temple University Press.

Klein, Ethel. 1984. *Gender Politics: From Consciousness to Mass Politics.* Cambridge, MA: Harvard University Press.

Koven, Seth and Sonya Michel. 1990. "Womanly Duties: Maternalist Politics and the Origins of Welfare States in France, Germany, Great Britain, and the United States, 1880–1920." *American Historical Review* 95(4):1076–108.

Kraditor, Aileen S. 1965. *The Ideas of the Women's Suffrage Movement, 1890–1920.* Garden City, NY: Anchor Books.

———, ed. 1968. *Up from the Pedestal.* New York: Quadrangle.

———. 1969. *Means and Ends in American Abolitionism.* New York: Vintage Books.

Lasch, Christopher. 1977. *Haven in a Heartless World.* New York: Basic Books.

Leach, Eugene E. 1993. "Social Reform Movements." Pp. 2201–30 in *Encyclopedia of American Social History,* edited by Mary K. Cayton, Elliott J. Gorn, and Peter W. Williams. New York: Scribner.

Lennon, Mary Clare and Sarah Rosenfield. 1994. "Relative Fairness and the Division of Housework: The Importance of Options." *American Journal of Sociology* 100(2):506–31.

Licata, Salvatore J. 1981. "The Homosexual Rights Movement in the United States." *Journal of Homosexuality* 6(1/2):161–89.

Lichterman, Paul. 1996. *The Search for Political Community: American Activists Reinventing Community.* Cambridge: Cambridge University Press.

Liebman, Robert C. and Robert Wuthnow, eds. 1983. *The New Christian Right.* Hawthorne, NY: Aldine.

Lorber, Judith. 1994. *Paradoxes of Gender.* New Haven, CT: Yale University Press.

Luker, Kristin. 1984. *Abortion and the Politics of Motherhood.* Berkeley: University of California Press.

Machung, Anne. 1989. "Talking Career, Thinking Job: Gender Differences in Career and Family Expectations of Berkeley Seniors." *Feminist Studies* 15(1):35–58.

Mansbridge, Jane J. 1986. *Why We Lost the ERA.* Chicago: University of Chicago Press.

———. 1993. "The Role of Discourse in the Feminist Movement." Paper presented at the annual meeting of the American Political Science Association, Washington, DC.

———. 1995. "What is the Feminist Movement?" Pp. 27–34 in *Feminist Organizations,* edited by Myra Marx Ferree and Patricia Yancey Martin. Philadelphia: Temple University Press.

Markson, Stephen L. 1982. "Normative Boundaries and Abortion Policy: The Politics of Morality." *Research in Social Problems and Public Policy* 2:21–33.

Mathews, Donald G. and Jane Sherron De Hart. 1990. *Sex, Gender, and the Politics of ERA.* New York: Oxford University Press.

Matlack, Carol. 1991. "Abortion Wars." *National Journal* 23(11):630–34.

May, Elaine Tyler. 1988. *Homeward Bound: American Families in the Cold War Era.* New York: Basic Books.

McAdam, Doug. 1982. *Political Process and the Development of Black Insurgency.* Chicago: University of Chicago Press.

———. 1988. *Freedom Summer.* New York: Oxford University Press.

Meyer, David S. and Nancy Whittier. 1994. "Social Movement Spillover." *Social Problems* 41:277–98.

Meyerowitz, Joanne. 1994. "Beyond the Feminine Mystique: A Reassessment of Postwar Mass Culture, 1946–1958." Pp. 229–62 in *Not June Cleaver: Women and Gender in Postwar America, 1945–1960,* edited by Joanne Meyerowitz. Philadelphia: Temple University Press.

Miller, James. 1987. *"Democracy Is in the Streets."* New York: Simon & Schuster.

Miller, Neil. 1995. *Out of the Past: Gay and Lesbian History from 1869 to the Present.* New York: Vintage Books.

Mintz, Steven and Susan Kellogg. 1988. *Domestic Revolutions: A Social History of American Family Life.* New York: Free Press.

Mohr, James C. 1978. *Abortion in America: The Origins and Evolution of National Policy.* New York: Oxford University Press.

Monthly Vital Statistics Report, Vol. 43(13), October 23, 1995.

Morgan, Robin, ed. 1970. *Sisterhood Is Powerful: An Anthology of Writings from the Women's Liberation Movement.* New York: Vintage Books.

Morris, Aldon D. 1984. *The Origins of the Civil Rights Movement.* New York: Free Press.

Morton, F. L. 1992. *Pro-Choice vs. Pro-Life: Abortion and the Courts in Canada.* Norman: University of Oklahoma Press.

Muller, Jerry Z. 1995. "The Conservative Case for Abortion." *The New Republic,* August 21 and 28, pp. 27–29.

Nasaw, David. 1985. *Children of the City: At Work and at Play.* New York: Oxford University Press.

Newsweek. 1990. "The Future of Gay America." March 12, pp. 20–27.

———. 1992. "Gays under Fire." September 14, pp. 35–40.

New York Times. 1995. "Shameless Homophobia and the 'Jenny Jones' Murder." March 19, section 4, p. 16.

———. 1996. "Gay Support for Clinton Holds in Middle America." September 22, p. 22.

Oberschall, Anthony. 1993. *Social Movements.* New Brunswick, NJ: Transaction.

Paige, Connie. 1983. *The Right to Lifers: Who They Are, How They Operate, Where They Get Their Money.* New York: Summit Books.

Peiss, Kathy. 1986. *Cheap Amusements: Leisure in Turn-of-the-Century New York.* Philadelphia: Temple University Press.

Petchesky, Rosalind P. 1984. *Abortion and Woman's Choice: The State, Sexuality and Reproductive Freedom.* Boston: Northeastern University Press.

———. 1989. "Change Strategies, Change Vision." *New Directions for Women* 18(5):1, 10.

Phelan, Shane. 1989. *Identity Politics: Lesbian Feminism and the Limits of Community.* Philadelphia: Temple University Press.

Pleck, Elizabeth H. 1993. "Gender Roles and Relations." Pp. 1945–60 in *Encyclopedia of American Social History,* edited by Mary K. Cayton, Elliott J. Gorn, and Peter W. Williams. New York: Scribner.

Renzetti, Claire M. 1987. "New Wave or Second Stage? Attitudes of College Women Toward Feminism." *Sex Roles* 16(5/6):265–77.

Reskin, Barbara and Irene Padavic. 1994. *Women and Men at Work.* Thousand Oaks, CA: Pine Forge Press.

Robnett, Belinda. 1996. "African-American Women in the Civil Rights Movement, 1954–1965: Gender, Leadership, and Micromobilization." *American Journal of Sociology* 101(6):1661–93.

Rubin, Eva. 1986. *The Supreme Court and the American Family: Ideology and Issues.* New York: Greenwood Press.

Rucht, Dieter. 1996. "The Impact of National Contexts on Social Movement Structures: A Cross-Movement and Cross-National Comparison." Pp. 185–204 in *Comparative Perspectives on Social Movements*, edited by Doug McAdam, John D. McCarthy, and Mayer N. Zald. New York: Cambridge University Press.

Rupp, Leila J. and Verta Taylor. 1987. *Survival in the Doldrums: The American Women's Rights Movement, 1945 to the 1960s.* New York: Oxford University Press.

Ryan, Barbara. 1992. *Feminism and the Women's Movement.* New York: Routledge.

Sale, Kirkpatrick. 1973. *SDS.* New York: Vintage Books.

Schneider, Beth E. 1987. "Feminist Disclaimers, Stigma, and the Contemporary Women's Movement." Paper presented at the annual meeting of the American Sociological Association, Chicago.

Scott, Joan W. 1986. "Gender: A Useful Category of Historical Analysis." *American Historical Review* 91(5):1053–75.

Segal, Lynne and Mary McIntosh, eds., 1992. *Sex Exposed: Sexuality and the Pornography Debate.* New Brunswick, NJ: Rutgers University Press.

Shilts, Randy. 1982. *The Mayor of Castro Street: The Life and Times of Harvey Milk.* New York: St. Martin's Press.

Shorter, Edward. 1975. *The Making of the Modern Family.* New York: Basic Books.

Shreve, Anita. 1989. *Women Together, Women Alone.* New York: Fawcett Columbine.

Simonds, Wendy. 1996. *Abortion at Work: Ideology and Practice in a Feminist Clinic.* New Brunswick, NJ: Rutgers University Press.

Sinclair, Andrew. 1965. *The Better Half: The Emancipation of American Women.* New York: Harper & Row.

Skolnick, Arlene. 1991. *Embattled Paradise: The American Family in an Age of Uncertainty.* New York: Basic Books.

Smith-Rosenberg, Carroll. 1975. "The Female World of Love and Ritual." *Signs* 1:1–29.

———. 1985. *Disorderly Conduct: Visions of Gender in Victorian America.* New York: Alfred A. Knopf, 1985.

Stacey, Judith. 1990. *Brave New Families: Stories of Domestic Upheaval in Late Twentieth Century America.* New York: Basic Books.

Staggenborg, Suzanne. 1987. "Life-style Preferences and Social Movement Recruitment: Illustrations from the Abortion Conflict." *Social Science Quarterly* 68:779–97.

———. 1991. *The Pro-Choice Movement: Organization and Activism in the Abortion Conflict.* New York: Oxford University Press.

———, Donna Eder, and Lori Sudderth. 1993–94. "Women's Culture and Social Change: Evidence from the National Women's Music Festival." *Berkeley Journal of Sociology* 38:31–56.

Sullivan, Andrew. 1996a. "Let Gays Marry." *Newsweek*, June 3, p. 26.

————. 1996b. "When AIDS Ends." *New York Times Magazine,* November 10, pp. 52–62, 76–77, 84.

Swerdlow, Amy. 1993. *Women Strike for Peace: Traditional Motherhood and Radical Politics in the 1960s.* Chicago: University of Chicago Press.

Szasz, Andrew. 1994. *Ecopopulism: Toxic Waste and the Movement for Environmental Justice.* Minneapolis: University of Minnesota Press.

Tarrow, Sidney. 1994. *Power in Movement: Social Movements, Collective Action, and Mass Politics in the Modern State.* Cambridge: Cambridge University Press.

Taylor, Verta. 1996. *Rock-a-by Baby: Feminism, Self-Help, and Postpartum Depression.* New York: Routledge.

———— and Leila J. Rupp. 1993. "Women's Culture and Lesbian Feminist Activism: A Reconsideration of Cultural Feminism." *Signs* 19(1):32–61.

———— and Marieke Van Willigen. 1996. "Women's Self-Help and the Reconstruction of Gender: The Postpartum Support and Breast Cancer Movements." *Mobilization* 1(2):123–42.

Tedin, K. L., D. W. Brady, M. E. Buxton, B. M. Gorman, and J. L. Thompson. 1977. "Social Background and Political Differences between Pro- and Anti-ERA Activists." *American Political Quarterly* 5(July):395–408.

Thomas, David J. 1986. "The Gay Quest for Equality in San Francisco." Pp. 27–41 in *The Egalitarian City,* edited by Janet K. Boles. New York: Praeger.

Thorne, Barrie. 1975. "Women in the Draft Resistance Movement: A Case Study of Sex Roles and Social Movements." *Sex Roles* 1(2):179–95.

Tilly, Charles. 1984. "Social Movements and National Politics." Pp. 297–317 in *Statemaking and Social Movements,* edited by Charles Bright and Susan Harding. Ann Arbor: University of Michigan Press.

————. 1995. *Popular Contention in Great Britain, 1758–1834.* Cambridge, MA: Harvard University Press.

Tilly, Louise A. and Joan W. Scott. 1978. *Women, Work, and Family.* New York: Holt, Rinehart and Winston.

Tong, Rosemarie. 1989. *Feminist Thought: A Comprehensive Introduction.* Boulder, CO: Westview Press.

Trebay, Guy. 1990. "In Your Face!" *Village Voice,* August 14, pp. 34–39.

U.S. Department of Commerce, Bureau of the Census. 1989. *Historical Statistics of the United States: Colonial Times to 1970.* White Plains, NY: Kraus International.

————. 1995. *Statistical Abstract of the United States.* Washington, DC: Author.

Vance, Carole S., ed. 1984. *Pleasure and Danger: Exploring Female Sexuality.* Boston: Routledge and Kegan Paul.

Vogel, Lise. 1995. *Woman Questions.* London: Pluto Press.

Ware, Susan. 1982. *Holding Their Own: American Women in the 1930s.* Boston: Twayne.

——. 1989. *American Women: A Documentary History.* Chicago: Dorsey Press.

Warner, Judith. 1993. "Mixed Messages." *Ms.,* November/December, pp. 21–25.

Welter, Barbara. 1966. "The Cult of True Womanhood: 1820–1860." *American Quarterly* 18:151–74.

Wertheimer, Barbara M. 1977. *We Were There: The Story of Working Women in America.* New York: Pantheon Books.

Whittier, Nancy. 1995. *Feminist Generations.* Philadelphia: Temple University Press.

——, Verta Taylor, and Jo Reger. 1995. "Gender and Social Movements." Paper presented at the annual meeting of the American Sociological Association, Washington, DC.

Wuthnow, Robert. 1986–87. "American Democracy and the Democratization of American Religion." *Politics and Society* 15(2):223–34.

Index

A

Abalone Alliance, 48

Abolition movement, 35-38

Abortion:

abortion rights (pro-choice)
movement, 71, 72, 75-80, 85-97

adolescents, 75, 76, 83, 84-85, 96-97

and capital punishment, 78

and contraception, 75, 76, 82-83, 85-86,
88, 96-97

and divorce, 75, 76, 78

and education, 72, 73, 76-78

and employment, 72, 74, 75-78, 82, 83

and euthanasia, 78

and family relations, 72, 75-76, 77, 79,
80-81, 82-83, 84-85, 87, 88-91,
94-95, 96-97

and government interference, 87-88

and homosexuality, 76, 78, 91

and income, 72, 74, 76, 77-78

and lifestyle/sexual behavior, 71-72,
75-78, 80-81, 82-83, 84-85, 90-91,
96-97

and military, 78

and morality/values, 71, 75-78, 79,
80-81, 82-83, 84-85, 87, 88-90, 96-97

and pornography, 75, 76, 78, 91

and rape, 76, 92

and religion, 72, 73, 76, 77, 78-79,
80-85, 87-88, 93, 94-96, 126

and sex education, 75, 76, 83, 88

and women's movement, 1, 75, 76-78,
80, 82-84, 86-88, 90-92

anti-abortion (pro-life) movement, 10,
71-75, 76, 77-85, 90-97, 124, 126

birth defects, 76, 126

Britain, 72

Canada, 79-81, 94-95

civil rights activists, 79, 80, 94-95

common concerns, 90-92

Equal Rights Amendment (ERA), 77

family heritage activists, 79, 80-81,
94-95

funding, 95, 96

gender roles of women, 72, 73-78,
82-83, 84-85, 88-89, 91, 96-97

historical/social context, 72-75

individual choice, 87-88, 90, 91, 95

lower class, 71, 95-96

men's concern with, 73-76, 80, 81-82,
84, 96

middle class, 71, 73, 89, 97

New Christian Right, 79, 84-85, 95-96

polarization, 92-96

pro-choice family values, 88-90

reproductive rights, 90, 95-96

revivalist Catholics, 79, 81, 94-95

Roe v. Wade, 82, 93

symbolism of, 71-78

true womanhood ideology, 73-75, 82

Abortion and the Politics of Motherhood
(Luker), 72

Acker, J., 2

Acquired Immune Deficiency Syndrome
(AIDS), 111, 113, 129

ACT UP. *See* AIDS Coalition to Unleash
Power

Adam, B., 99, 108, 109, 110, 111, 112, 113,
116, 117, 119